The Girl who Died at 7

Victoria Necole

First Printing: September
2017 Victoria N. Long
Birmingham, AL 35209 www.VictorianLong.com

Ordering Information:
Quantity sales. Special discounts are available on quantity purchases by corporations, associations, and others. For details, contact the publisher at the address above.
Orders by U.S. trade bookstores and wholesalers. Please contact Victoria N. Long: Tel: 205.538.0731 or visit www.victorianlong.com.

Printed in the United

States of America

ISBN-13:978-1548504113

DEDICATION

This book is dedicated to all the little girls
that died before their time because they had to
live a complex adult life as a child. For those of
you who lost a part of themselves and feel that
they can't get it back; I am here to tell you that
you can, and you will live again. There's
no one holding you back now but yourself.
Cheers to a bright and beautiful today and
forevermore.

TABLE OF CONTENTS

Acknowledgment
Foreword

ACKNOWLEDGMENTS

Insert First and foremost, I want to acknowledge God. Thank you for not allowing me to give up on myself because there is greater purpose and work for me to do here on earth.

To my little mini Kaytlyn "Lady" Delani. Mommy loves you more than you will ever know. Regardless of which way the wind blows, I am always right there with you. You are my happiness, peace and joy. Life will come with its obstacles and you will feel defeated, but just know we will make it together and do it as animated as possible. Mommy loves you.

For my best friend Nautica, I don't know where my life would be if I didn't have you in it. You are a living angel. Please remember that nothing you have done for me has gone in vain. Thank you for being the best friend a person could ever think of. I often think to myself that I couldn't have prayed for a better Godmother for Delani. You are the peanut butter to this jelly and the yang to my yang.

To my mother for allowing me to be just me, I love you unconditionally. Our relationship hasn't been the best, but I know you did the all that you could with what you had. Never think for a minute that I take anything you've done for me for granted. I get my hustle and ambition from you.

To my big brother for always being a voice of reason, and shoulder to cry on. Words can never express, and actions can never show how much you truly mean to Lady and me. I know you say it's because we're family but at the end of the day we love us some Big Brother/ Uncle D.

On that day in October 2010 I knew my life would never be the same. I was still broken and torn into a million of pieces. Lady J you never held my hand and always made me acknowledge where my pain was coming from. Even when I wanted to give up you wouldn't allow it to be so. You would say "stand right here and scream and yell it out you're going to be just fine" ...Unlike so many you know what you're supposed to do and when you're ready you will get it right." You are truly one of the reasons I am who I am today. You never judged me or held my past against me. No matter how many times I made mistake and wen backwards you were right there. No matter where life takes me your words of encouragement will always be with me.

Momma Raby thank you staying on the phone with me late nights and early mornings when the spirit of depression would consume me. Thank you for your continuous prayers.

Dee you're been trying to read me from the day I bought your book and I thank you for it. There are few people that I let in with full trust from the beginning. Thank you for being there through these many transitions...

Noisha thank you for being my spiritual protector. My "see here's the thing about it" friend." I know God ordained this friendship please know that I value and cherish you more than you know. You've truly helped me grow.

Teresa and KD I thank you guys for helping me through this process. I know you wanted to throw your computers so many times, but I thank you for sticking out his journey with me.

FOREWARD

Imagine being told that YOUR body is not your own. Imagine shaking with fear as your mother leaves for work and you hear "him" come toward your room.

You hold your breath as he whispers, "Are you asleep?" Did I mention that you have yet to reach your 10th birthday?

Chances are if you are preparing to read this book you or someone you know have been through something in your life at a young age. Maybe you are the parent of a young child and you want to make sure that you don't miss the potential signs that they are going through something. Maybe you are unaware of the epidemic of childhood sexual abuse and the effects it has on the victims and the title of this book caught your eye.

As someone who has been in the social service field for over 10 years let me tell you it's real. The girl you call a slut, the young boy you label as aggressive, the adult that suffers with PTSD they may all be victims of sexual abuse. According to RAINN every 98 seconds American is sexually abused or assaulted and every 8 minutes the victim is a child however only 6 out of 1000 perpetrators go to jail.

Sexual abuse and other topics mentioned in this book are taboo, especially to our community. But you can open your mind and heart the way Victoria did through her clever use of words and imagery in this book. Let her experiences set you on the path to healing. Whether that be healing of your past abuse or healing of how you treated those who have been abused. This book is a gift, read it as such.

When you read this book allow yourself to become the character. Fully understand the pain and the hurt she is feeling. Then read it again and resume being yourself, a bystander, thinking about others you know in similar situations as the main character.

Examine every negative thought you have had about that person. Replay every statement of judgment, every nasty looks you gave and every inch of your nose that you looked down. Forgive the person that you were and walk into the person this book will transform you to be.

Education is the eraser of ignorance!

Katesha
"KD"
Reid
Freedom
Strategist

Victoria Necole

INTRODUCTION

The Girl Who Died at 7 is a story about factual events that shaped a young lady's life and impacted the decisions, interactions, and paths that she chose throughout her childhood, teenage years, and adulthood. While some may view these stories as acts of desperation or opportunities to seek attention, others may view them as indicators that something went severely wrong somewhere down this young lady's lifetime.

This is not a story that you give to a child for bedtime or daytime reading and it certainly isn't a story that you give to a child that hasn't been exposed to things beyond their years. I think this is the perfect story however, to allow adults as well as some children that have been exposed to molestation, abuse, domestic violence, sexual activity and promiscuity to read in hopes they will see how certain events could possibly have an impact on future decisions and even frame the way you view your life.

I hope that this story makes people aware of being less judgmental and critical of our youth and make us as a community more responsible for their safety and well – being. I pray that parents read this book and understand that our children need us. They need love, discipline, structure, guidance, positive reinforcement, listening ears and most importantly reassurance that we are holding them accountable for their actions.

You can never be sure of what another child has been exposed to so don't be so quick to pass your child off to other people's household and environments. Be aware, attentive, and never assume anything when it comes to your children.

We have one opportunity to set the foundation, so our kids don't take life for granted

You will never make it try to be someone else!
-Victoria Necole

1 WHO AM I

Insert Who am I? It's amazing how three small words can hold so much weight and value. When thinking about it, these three small words can cause you to go from appearing confident to displaying a vast amount of uncertainty. Who am I? So simple yet so complex. On the surface, you may think my answer is, "I'm Victoria, daughter of Michael and Shirley. I have two brothers and one sister. I was born in Kansas, but raised in Florida," but that's only the surface of who I am. Who I am today reflects the interactions I have had in my past and how I took these experiences to build a better future for me, my child, and as many people as I can encourage and guide along the way.

Molestation, domestic violence, abuse of all kinds, a psychiatric stay, attempted rape, sexing the crew, prostitution, tricking my friends, suicide attempts and that was the real me. That period of my life marked events and changes that took place and shaped my views and behaviors; Moments and times where things took pivotal turns, mainly for the worse.

Today, year 2018, if you ask me how I define myself I say, I am a lover of God who used to be a sex addict. Think Janet Jackson's song *Anytime, Anyplace,* add the remix of "Anybody" and you had me. Who am I? Although I was a sex addict, I didn't see myself as one of "them," those other sex addicts because I had standards. To be graced with all Vic had to offer you had to be willing to pay to play. I had to benefit from you and I am not speaking physically because, what was a simple orgasm? No, I required car note payments, rent checks, meals, trips, clothes, shoes, you name it and I accepted it. So now you see why asking "Who am I" is so complex. If you asked me then I would have proudly said I was a woman who was in control and someone who used what she had to get what she wanted. Looking back at that same woman, I realize I was lost, my values where slim, my identity was complex, and my purpose was yet to be discovered.

The funny thing is, although I wasn't clear on who I was, I had a strong inclination that I wouldn't always be that way. During my mess, I knew my actions were wrong. Every time I went in to these various situations I knew I was wrong which let me know somewhere deep inside I didn't want to continue living this way, but today in 2017 when asked who I am, I can confidently say, "I am Victoria, I am a child of God and I am a Christian who truly loves the Lord." As you read this book be aware that this is an account of my story and it will not be about how I knew the Lord all my life and trusted in His divine plan. Better yet it will be about how The Lord loved me, how He saved me repeatedly and how He kept me despite my issues.

Yes, you will see that his arm is not to short and no matter how far you go you will never be out of reach from God him. I am a living testimony.

2 WAFFLES

My entire life I've been told, "Victoria, there's something different about you." I never understood what that meant or what they were trying to say. I never felt different so what exactly where people referring to? Then came 7. One day as we sat on my grandmother's brown, smoke infested couch, slightly slumped to the left and placed next to the floor model television, I stared at her attentively as she told me what to do. "Climb up on me and place your hand right here," she said, as she pointed toward her breast.

This was a female family member who cared for me when my mother wasn't around. I guess she felt my hesitation or saw the fear in my eyes because she replied, "If you do what I tell you, I will let you have the leftover waffles that are in the refrigerator." Although I wasn't hungry, and her proposition gave me no comfort, I couldn't say no to her. I remember looking at how sad she looked.

I told myself, "Just do it, it will all be over soon," after all I was raised to obey adults without question. I felt stuck between a rock and a hard place, so I just did it. I did exactly what she instructed me to do.

I climbed my seven-year-old body on top of her and took her fully grown breast into my mouth kissing and licking it all while she was rubbing on me. The thought of this is disgusting, but she moaned. I had no idea what that meant, so I continued kissing and licking until she told me to stop. "This is our little secret and no one can know," she said to me, "no one would believe you anyway, now go to the fridge and get the waffles." I stood there with the door open and stated at the styrofoam container. I wasn't hungry earlier, and I wasn't hungry now. Not wanting to disappoint her, I reached in the drawer, grabbed a fork and proceeded to break off a piece of waffle and place it in my mouth. It was wet and soggy, so much so that I became sick to my stomach and couldn't finish it. I put it in the trash and hid it in the plastic   bag.

I wish I could tell you from here on out my life turned into a fairytale and this was a one-time incident, but that is far from the truth. Unlike most children, I didn't have a constant reminder that I was safe and loved. Having the comfort of adults who would never treat me wrong was foreign to me. Unconditional love wasn't something I had ever been afforded. Knowing that greater was in my future, but lacking these basic foundational needs proved to be a hard road to travel.

At an early age, my body had begun to shape and mature at a different rate than my peers. At eight, I developed breasts and at 10 I noticed I had curves and a roundness to my bottom. Unknowing to me my body was also changing internally, I had my first cycle.

Imagine waking up at 10 to your cute panties, you know the ones with the pink hearts on them, being full of blood. What did I do to deserve this? God am I dying? Why was I in so much pain? We recently learned about body development at school, but not once did it cross my mind that I would be experiencing this at the tender age of 10.

I had no clue what to do, and I wondered if I should tell my mom. I feared that she would yell at me or be upset. I had to decide because the blood was not stopping. As it continued to flow down my legs I walked up the hallway. Every squeak felt like I had walked a mile down our trailer to the kitchen where my mom was cooking.

"Momma I need to talk

to you..." "What is it

Victoria?"

I pulled my panties from behind my back and said what is this? "Oh my God!" she said, as she rolled her eyes, "Ugh! You're too young. Go to your bathroom I will be in there in a minute."

As I sat on the toilet, I felt so ashamed as if I had done something wrong. I knew I shouldn't have told her, but I had no choice. I began to cry. My mother entered the bathroom shortly and placed the maxi pad in my panties and said, "Well now you know you can get pregnant." What? I thought as I looked at her with amazement. I don't even know how to get pregnant. I don't want to get pregnant. Before I could ask any questions, she left and returned to the kitchen. I sat there for a moment. The pains worsened. I questioned myself thinking, is there already something in there, when will this stop?

As I walked to the kitchen to talk to my mom about what I was experiencing, I overheard her on the phone with my granny saying, "Mom guess what? Victoria just got her cycle. Ugh! I hope she isn't nasty with it, you know I can't stand the smell of it. I told her she could get pregnant now." I immediately did an about face, went back in my room and cried myself to sleep.

Ashamed, embarrassed, and mortified are all appropriate words to describe how I felt. I wanted to go away and never come back, I wanted to die. I was so frustrated that I scratched my face in rage and yanked on my hair. This would mark the first time I inflicted pain on myself.

All I wanted was answers and guidance. I mean that's what your mommy is for, right? She was an adult and had been pregnant, so surely, she had gone through this before. Being afraid was scary, but her reaction caused me to feel judged, confused and alone. I still had questions, so I reached out to the next person I could think of, my teacher.

When I got to school, I explained to my teacher that I wasn't feeling well. "Can you come to the bathroom with me, so I can tell you what's going on?" The look on her face was like the look I must have made when my mom informed me I could now get pregnant, but she agreed to come. "I don't feel well, my mom said I can get pregnant now, I don't want to have any children right now because I am not old enough to have them." She had a look of concern on her face and words of compassion on her lips. "Having children right now shouldn't be on your mind," she   assured   me.

"Your mommy is just afraid because her little girl is growing up and maturing."

Reflecting on this part of my life makes me realize that it's not only how we communicate with our children, but how we respond to them. Our children's world and our adult world may not always be the same, but children still have valid concerns and problems. Many times, as adults we may be so wrapped up in "adulting" that we don't take the time to breathe and pay full attention to our kids when they need us the most. We may even think to ourselves that our kids are being "dramatic," but I believe it's better to pay attention and treat their concerns genuinely than to dismiss them and cause our children to have to reach out to strangers or end up in predicaments that they shouldn't be in. Be mindful of who you are leaving your children with, be it family or friends. Children are highly suggestive and can sometimes be manipulated in a way that put them in situations that can be harmful. Give your child a voice. Ask them how their day went and what happened while they are wherever you left them.

I know I will be great at whatever life throws at me, but the process sucks!

-Victoria Necole

3 WELCOME TO ATALANTA

Insert As life begins to get the best of me, I thought it would be better if I went to live with my dad. I was unhappy with my home life and I thought surely my dad's house couldn't be like this. I believe my mom gave in because somewhere in her mind she was already tired of me, so why not? However, what I found out in a short four months is that this wasn't the greatest idea.

Despite everything that ever happened to me, I will always admire that my mother never spoke ill about my dad or any of my sibling's dads. She would always say, "In due time you will find out who they are." I didn't think one way or the other about that comment.

I went to live with my dad in Atlanta (ATL). The move proved to be a huge culture shock to the little girl from Kansas and everything I was accustomed to. My dad welcomed me into his home, if you would call it that. It was more like a room inside of a house that he shared with several other people. My first night there I slept in his bed and he slept on the couch in the room. Scared is an understatement. I began to doubt my decision.

My parents separated when I was a toddler and legally divorced when I was 10, so I was just meeting him and now we were sharing a room! I hardly slept that first night. When my body finally did relax I was awakened to my father shaking the bed. I had no idea what was going on. He appeared to have been drinking, he was trying to get up, but could not catch his balance. Struggling to lay as still as I possibly could I could not stop the tears from falling. What had I gotten myself into? Is this what my mom was protecting me from? I called his name and he looked up at me as though he had forgotten I was in the room. "Go back to sleep," he said, "I'm okay." I couldn't sleep because I was worried about him. Lord please don't let him hurt himself trying to get up. I was used to a lot of things, but this was not one of them. My mother wasn't much of a drinker. I remember her having wine coolers in the house for weeks before half the case would even be gone.

Just like with my mom I found one thing that I could not deny admiring about my dad, he knew how to work for what he wanted. I imagine this is what drew them together. My mom had many jobs throughout the years to make sure my siblings and I had everything we needed. Wants were another story, but we did not lack any necessities.

My dad and I didn't stay at the shared house for long. A couple of weeks later we moved into a 2-bedroom apartment. I was so excited to have my own room, this was something I hadn't had at my mother's home in a very long time. I was overwhelmed with the privacy I now had.

My Dad worked at Friday's and since I didn't know anyone in the city, I would go and sit there for hours waiting for him to get off. Luckily, he had a coworker that had a daughter my age and she and I became friends. Finally, I could do something other than waiting countless hours on my dad to get off. I learned to ride the Marta bus to hang out with her and her friends. Summer had arrived and to say it was interesting would be an understatement. We hung out all night, went to the movies and crossed paths with many pretty boys. It was official! I had a thing for pretty boys. Well-groomed fitted clothing, fresh smell of recent showers, mustaches neatly trimmed, low cut fades or braids. Yes!

And there was not a shortage of them. They were unlike boys back in Florida.

Okay let's continue, I just had a moment.

Told you I'm not perfect, just kept by grace.

Have you ever had a friend who had a brother that was friends with all the fine boys? That was my girl Cynt. We hung out at her house daily during the summer. Her brother wasn't too fond of us being there because he knew his friends and their intentions. Cynt didn't care, so we didn't care. I later found out she was sleeping with one of his friends. As the summer was coming to an end all the girls were hooking up with guys except me.

I was used to it. Where I was from no one really paid any attention, so being in a new city I didn't expect anything different. I enjoyed being in the background, sex wasn't really an option for me. I planned to wait until I got married. I mean that is all they preached to us in teen church so surely it was the right thing to do. "Save yourself until marriage," they would say repeatedly. However, no one explained all the temptation that would come while waiting.

With two weeks left in the summer I met Ant. Brown skinned with short curly hair that he kept well moisturized, (as he walked close to me I could see the sun beaming off his head. Is his head going to catch on fire, I would think to myself, this Atlanta heat is no joke)? He walked up to me one day and spoke. I was in disbelief. I'm not even sure if I spoke back. Cynt formally introduced us and informed him that I had just moved here with my dad from Florida and that I wasn't living on this side of town. She even told him how we met and that I spent a lot of time with her. I was so nervous I felt and sounded nervous and I know I probably looked nervous. I could barely look him in the face.

He would ask me questions and I would stare off. He begins to pick with me, "You don't sound like a Florida girl, you too proper."

Little did he know this has always been a trigger for me. I became very defensive. Being from the Midwest there weren't a lot of little girls that looked like me in my class. My classmates would call me an Oreo and ask, "Why do you talk that way? Not knowing what they meant, I began to question   myself.

Although I had given him my home number, we didn't speak on the phone much and only saw each other a few times after that.

I was so excited for school to start. Not only did I enjoy school, but in my mind the beginning of school would be my chance to make more friends. My excitement quickly turned to worry. What was I supposed to wear? They dressed different from what I was used to. My first impression was, "Is this a fashion show or are we here to learn?" Everyone and everything just seemed so different. We had to walk through metal detectors. As I leaned over to ask the security guard why we had
to do this he yelled out, "Oh, you must be new, let me see your purse."

Once again, a feeling of embarrassment overcame me as I was on my cycle. Please don't let my pads fall out, please don't let my pads fall out. Last thing I needed was to be embarrassed on top of already not feeling well.

Girls at the school were way more advanced than I was or even cared to be. Half of them were already sexually active and had babies as well as numerous sex partners. The guys were not any better. I often

wondered if they could sense I was a virgin and saw me as a challenge. Guys would walk down the hall and make sexual comments toward me. Coming from a place where no attention was paid to me, I often found myself shocked they were even speaking to me. School was a culture shock.

Lunch was no different. There were so many students in one place. They were grouped up, and very loud and disrespectful to one another. Lunch period appeared to be a source of entertainment. Security officers lined the walls and all I could think to myself was, "Why do they have all these officers? Are the kids here really that bad? Why did they have to be policed during lunch time?" My moment of questioning was interrupted as I saw Ant. He didn't speak to me nor was he walking my way. He was leaning over talking to another female.

"Don't worry girl, that's his on again, off again girlfriend." Cynt said "it's nothing major, don't even worry about him."

"Girl I'm not," I replied. "She looks loose and if that is what he likes, oh well I'm not trying to make him my boyfriend anyway."

The truth was I couldn't help but worry about him. He was the first guy that paid me any attention and to see him in the face of another girl hurt.

As I began to think to myself well there went another one, I felt someone staring at me.

"Cynt what's up with her, do you know her?" "Yeah, we used to be friends until she...turned." "Turned?

What does that mean?" I asked.

She laughed like she always did when I didn't understand their slang.

"Turned, you know, like she has a girlfriend and she likes girls."

Still not understanding I asked for more clarification. "You're a girl and you're my friend Cynt." "No not like that, Victoria you're so green!" there was that laugh again.

"She likes girls and it all came out this summer."

Cynt didn't know about my childhood and what happened to me. And although I wasn't really into girls, I was confused about what had taken place and I never told anyone how it made me feel and how I had been curious to explore more.

Now there is no way I would ever tell her this.

Later that day I bumped into the girl that had been staring at me during lunch.

"What's your name? I'm Shawn."

I introduced myself to her. Shawn was pretty. A little taller than me, 5'3 no more than 126 lbs. She had long black hair and a small waist. She was shaped like me. I didn't understand why people were so mean to her. So, what she had turned or whatever they were saying. Within the few moments she and I were speaking people kept walking by turning up their faces. Some even called her a hoe under their fake coughs.

"Why are they treating you like this?" I asked.

"I don't know," she said, "The rumor is that I like girls and I have a stud as a girlfriend."

For some reason there was a moment of silence. "Are you okay?" she asked

"I'm not from here and I don't really understand what you mean by stud and girlfriend."

"Here, here's my number we can talk about it over the phone one day," she said as she wrote her number on my notebook.

I gave her my number and headed to class. Before I could get in my seat good Cynt walked up to me, "Why you talking to Shawn? People are going to think that you like girls."

This day began to get overwhelming. To top it off I rushed to class and forgot to bring my supplies.

"May I borrow a pencil?" I whispered to the teacher.

"You guys keep coming to class without any supplies. Why do you come to school if you are not prepared to learn?" she said out loud to the class.

I tried to explain to the teacher that this was my first time and it was an honest mistake.

"Be quiet, find a pencil on your own!" she yelled back. With her unnecessary rudeness on top of everything else. I was so ready for the weekend.

When I think back on this part of my life, it makes me realize that as a child you may think you know what's best for you, but you really don't. This move to Atlanta was way too advanced for me. With proper supervision and guidance, things may have turned out another way, but even with the smallest opportunities to a young and curious mind, those opportunities may lead to a road that no one including parents are ready for. Prepare your kids, guide your kids, and communicate about entering new situations. Most importantly listen to them and don't assume that they are grown simply because they can feed, clothe, bathe themselves, and make a few mature decisions.

No one likes rejection, but sometimes it's necessary.
-Victoria Necole

4 THAT ONE TIME

I was never the most popular girl in school. For as long as I can remember, I was bullied. Growing up I had a huge gap in my mouth like my dad's and I was tormented by other kids who would sing the popular jingle, *Fall into the Gap* that was the worse. My social life in general was horrible because I never had any real friends. One day I became friends with the girl from up the block, but because I didn't have the latest fashions or spoke the way they did they called me an, "Oreo" or a black girl trapped in a white girl's body. Even to this day I never understood how children can be so mean.

After the abuse from my childhood, I thought the fondling and playing around with other girls was normal, especially when everyone's house that I spent the night over or even played with, was doing it. Yes, and I mean everyone. Now that I think back on it was I supposed to know that little girls shouldn't play with or touch other little girls in that matter.

What made matters worse for me is the boys in my high school didn't find me attractive because I was pretty, but because I had a "shape" they felt that it would be better to try to experiment sexually by fingering or having full blown sex. Allowing every boy that paid attention to me to have his way with me was not an option. I was walking in shame and guilt, but because no one knew about my encounter with girls I was more okay with that.

Shawn and I continued to be friends even though Cynt warned me that people would start assuming the worse because I was associating myself with her, but at this point I didn't care and curiosity had gotten the best of me. She invited me over to her house and since my dad worked late I knew if I answered the phone when he called and beat him home, sneaking over to her house wouldn't be an issue; so, I went. Everything was fine at first until she offered me some wine. My first thought was where in the world did she get this and that she was trying to kill me. (I've always been over the top). I told her that I didn't want to become an alcoholic and that I had never drank wine before. She laughed at me with a strange look on her face. I don't know how we ended up in her mothers' room sitting on the bed talking. The next thing I know she had her hand up my shirt and asked me if I had ever been with another girl.

I told her, "No, but explain to me what she meant because I've kissed a girl and I fingered one, but that was about it."

She laughed again and said I will show you and she tried to pull down my pants. Everything in me wanted to get up and leave, but I didn't want to be rude or seem scary. See that was the thing about me I wanted to fit in so bad I would do anything to not make people get upset with me. She pulled down my pants. I stopped her and told her that I couldn't do this in the light. She looked at me with a confused look on her face and got up to close the curtain. I told her that was still too much light.

She suggested that we go into the bathroom because that was the only place that didn't have direct sunlight. The entire time I felt disgusted but pleased. However, she was a pro and there was no stopping her. I laid there, and I didn't know whether to cry or moan. When it was over I cleaned up and told her that I had to go. She sent me a text message later as I was walking to the bus stop and asked me how it was? I didn't want to lie and say I didn't enjoy it because I did physically more than I expected, but mentally I didn't know how to feel. I knew it wasn't right and I would never go back to her house. I would like to say that was my last time with a woman, but it wasn't, it was only the beginning.

That following Monday at school I felt she sent out a mass text message to everyone and they knew what took place. It was the guilt and paranoia that had me afraid to blink as if someone was out to get me.

It only takes one opportunity coupled with curiosity for children to fall into inappropriate situations. Now that I reflect on this part of my life I wonder what happened to this girl that would make her so sexually experienced as well as comfortable enough to not only drink wine but offer me some as well. We were in high school, yes, but we were only 15. Was she fondled with as a child, molested and or raped? Do her parents know she was into sex relations? She was probably as confused and tormented as I was.

Many parents are so excited that their children are out of the stage of having to be constantly watched that they fail to realize that even in teen stages you must watch them even more. I should have never had as much opportunity to get into the situations that I did. I understand that some parents desire to give their children "freedom" not realizing that "freedom" might lead them to destruction's door. Children need guidance and structure all throughout their developing stages and even after they are legally considered adults. You never know who you are leaving them with and what experiences that person(s) have had. Think about it and be wise. I should have stayed home, but curiosity got the best of me.

Every 98 seconds, an American is sexually assaulted and every 8 minutes that victim is a child.

Meanwhile, 6 out of every 1,000 perpetrators will end up in prison.

5 I WAS ONLY 15

Still in Atlanta, school was back in session on a Friday. I was standing outside the school waiting for Cynt to come out. She was very slow moving and took her time with everything. She was one of the more popular girls in school because she was for the most part very positive, smart and had a loving attitude. Like clockwork, every day after school the ice cream truck was parked across the street. I felt someone come and stand behind me. I turned around and there he was smiling and smelling good. I couldn't crack a frown if I wanted to. He asked me was I going to buy him some ice cream. I stared him right in the eye and told him I don't buy guys that have girlfriend's ice cream. He laughed and told me not to be that way and was that the reason I was ignoring him in the hallways when he tried to speak to me. Before I knew it, I pushed him and told him that he was a liar and I wasn't ignoring him that he had too much going on and I didn't want to get caught in any mess with any of his females. They already didn't like me, and I wasn't trying to give them another reason not to. He laughed and walked off.

The next day Cynt asked if she and her little sister could come over. I was so bored; my Dad was at work as usual and there weren't any girls my age in my apartment building, so I was excited to have company. It took them almost an hour to get there.

We walked to the store to get some candy. There were always guys standing on the corner doing God knows what. They were in their early twenties and would always pick with me when I walked passed. This time one broke out singing R. Kelly's, *It Seems Like You're Ready*. I turned to Cynt and asked her what in the world was he talking about? Ready for what? She laughed and told me to keep walking.

When we got back to the house Cynt called her friend that she met over the summer the same time I met Ant. She asked me did I mind him coming over and that he was going to bring Ant with him. I had this bad feeling in my stomach and I knew my dad would have a fit if he came home and saw guys were in the house, but I told her it was okay. Time had passed when I heard a tap at the door. It was Marc, (also known as Slew was told he got his name because he drugs his foot when he walked), and Ant. They walked in for a moment and then we all sat on the couch and started talking. Ant asked me if he could have something to drink since I didn't think about him when I went to the store.

While in the kitchen he walked up behind me and I could feel his penis on my butt. He leaned over and whispered in my ear, "Look what you did to me. You know you want this wearing those little shorts I know you put them on for me." I laughed and told him I had these on all day and they weren't put on for him. He laughed and started to kiss me on my neck. I turn around and told him that he needed to stop because he had a girlfriend. He pushed me up against the kitchen sink and told me that they weren't together anymore and that I need to worry about myself because he is with me right now. Ant had a way with words and I've had this crush on him all summer, but something about what he was trying to do didn't   feel   right.

I pushed him off me and tried to go back in the front room when he asked me to show him my room. I told him that wasn't going to happen. They were only supposed to come and chill and that involved staying in the living room. He walked up on me and told me that I needed to stop playing like a little girl all uptight and chill. In my mind I wanted everyone to leave, but I didn't want to be the outsider anymore either. I told him I had to go to the bathroom and by the time I got out, hopefully he would have calmed down. Everyone was looking like I had said something wrong.

I sat on the toilet contemplating if I wanted him to come in my room or not. I really liked Ant, but I hardly knew him. Maybe if I just let him come in nothing would happen, we would just talk, he would like me and see that I wasn't as green as everyone kept calling me and we would be okay but that thought just didn't sit right with me. Suddenly, I heard a tap at the door.

"Who is it?" I yelled

"Aye, can I come in?" I replied and said,

"No, can I please have some privacy?"

He laughed, and I looked under the door to see if he had left. I opened the door and there he was standing in the corner. He scared me, and I jumped back. He told me I can give you a massage to help you from being so uptight. I tried to walk past him when he grabbed me by my waist and started to walk me backwards.

"Ant will you please stop playing?"

I asked trying to push him back in the living room. The more I pushed, the more he pushed against me. I was becoming so nervous I tried to play fight with him to get him to fall in to the living room. Kicking, slapping, pinching nothing was working. He finally picked me up and carried me in my room.

He started to kiss me, and I didn't kiss him back. He told me to stop being so stubborn and just go with it. I told him that I wasn't being stubborn, and I didn't want it. With all his weight on top of me he stuck his hands down my shorts. I tried to wiggle him off me, but before I knew it he had a finger inside of me. I was terrified I didn't know what to do. He began to pull down his pants. I tried to move his hand and he pinned me back down. I closed my eyes and asked God if he would please make something happen to stop this. I could feel the tip of his penis enter when Cynt sister came knocking at the door and yelled your Dad is on the phone. Ant looked nervous and he got from on top of me. I ran to the door. My Dad told me he was on his way home, but he was stopping by the corner store and asked if I wanted anything. I was so relieved. I told everyone that my Dad was right down the street and they had to leave. That night I cried myself to sleep questioning how I allowed myself to get into this situation?

The next day I wrote my friend back home a letter telling her about what happened. I hid the notebook under my bed. A few days had passed by and when I came home from school my Dad was sitting at the table with a beer and my notebook in his hand. He asked me if there was anything that I needed to talk to him about. I instantly became defensive. Yelling and screaming at my dad I said, "If you have something to ask me just say it and don't start with all the games." I was so nervous. He looked at me and said, "Victoria I am your dad and you will not talk to me that way."

I screamed back and said, "Oh really?! I'm a teenager and you think you can tell me what to do. If it was left up to you, there would be no me living here so don't start with my dad mess."

He looked as if he wanted to cry, I didn't care. Mumbling, he said, "You are so rude, and you need to watch your mouth when you talk to me." Although I was being disrespectful I was in as much shock that he read my notebook as he probably was when he read it. He handed me the notebook and asked me what happened and who is the letter to? I began to yell and started to cry saying, "You went in my room rambling through my stuff. I have no privacy. I don't love you and I don't want to be here," I ran to my room, slammed and locked the door.

I was so angry. How could he come in my room and go through all my stuff? We hardly knew each other, and this was a total violation. I felt that I had only two options, act as if nothing happened or call my mother and tell her my side of the story before he did. Life in Atlanta was officially terrible, and I didn't want to be there, and I didn't want to see Ant again. Going to school and having people think that he and I slept together wasn't an option either.

My Dad was in the bathroom when I snuck the phone in my room, called my mom and told her what happened. She was so upset and told me I knew better than to have company in the house in the first place. My dad wasn't ready to be a parent because he was too busy trying to be my friend. She told me she was coming to get me that night. I took the phone to my Dad. He looked like he was in utter disbelief that I told her. He begged my mother not to come and get me and that this wouldn't happen again. My mother had her mind made up.

When he hung up he looked at me and said, "I would have never told your mother what happened and risk not having you in my life again." My mother arrived early the next morning and she and my dad had a few words. She told us that I would never come back to Georgia until I was an adult because I couldn't handle the city life. As I walked away I looked back at my dad's tears ran down his face. He stood in the doorway of his building until we were out of site. I was so young. It seemed to be one situation after another one. I can't believe I was almost raped at the age of 15.

As I reflect, I have asked myself several questions. Why didn't Cynt just stay home with her sister and invite her guy friend over to her house? Was this part of the hook up? Not only that, but all of this was going down with a younger child in the house. This could have ended up bad in so many ways, but God. It seemed cool now to have the freedom to have some friends over without permission, but now I see why my dad told me not to have company at the house while he wasn't there. In hindsight what other reason would these guys be coming over for? I was not as mature as I thought I was. I wasn't ready for all the freedom that city life had to bring. I know can see why my mom kept me on a short leach and didn't allow me to have the same freedom as the other girls in my class. Years, later I sit and thank God that nothing came of that day!

Victoria Necole

What's waiting for you on the other side?

-Victoria Necole

6 PUPPY LOVE

Have you ever dealt with someone that you knew was trouble from the moment you laid eyes on them? But you somehow convinced yourself to give them a chance anyway? Well, that was me. I said to myself that maybe I shouldn't be so hard on everyone and that I should be nice for a change. This decision was the beginning of what I call puppy love. I knew this guy was nothing to play with and I was pretty sure that dealing with him was going to end in trouble, but I was okay with that.

I had only been in the "A" for a couple of months, but when I came back the neighborhood was different. Everyone was doing the most for the least cause. It was as if everyone got a hold of the, "ochie coochie" juice and all my so-called friends were giving and receiving the seafood platter or speaking into the microphone. The Nokia's with the snake game on them had just come out and calls were just now becoming free after 9.

Now I will be the first to admit that I had no business falling for this guy the way I did. You know that guy that everyone in the neighborhood wants, but for some reason he only wants you. By now you should know that I was not the girl that was sought after. No one was really checking for me, so when he approached me, I was taken aback.

I had my guard up and I can remember asking him why in the world he was trying to talk to me? He had this sad puppy look on his face as if he wasn't getting ready to wreak havoc upon me and turn my entire world upside down. It was at that moment I should have run for the hills and never looked back, but nope I wanted to be grown, explore and go against my better judgement.

I gave him my number. We would stay up all night talking and texting. On Sundays, he and all his friends would go to the court and play basketball and me and my friend Drea would sneak and watch them before my brother would yell and tell me to go home. Thinking back, I should have listened to my brother more than I did. A few days had passed, I sent PL a text to bring me an orange Sunkist soda. I remember being at home laying on a mattress in the middle of the living room floor. My mother was at work, my baby sister and brother were gone, and my older brother had left the house through the backdoor. He came over and we sat there in the middle of the floor talking.

I asked/accused him of talking to one of the other girls in the neighborhood and we had a small argument and that's when he leaned over to kiss me. This time I wasn't scared like I was with Ant. He tried to take my pants down when I told him to stop. He asked me was I sure and I told him, "Yes I didn't want my first time to be on the mattress on the floor of my mother's living room." He replied by telling me it was best if he left because he didn't want to feel as if he was pressuring me into doing something I didn't want to do. I agreed and that was the last time I saw him for several months.

PL was a good boy from a decent family, but he chose to run the streets. After that day at the house he had gotten into a fight with someone at his school and was sent to detention. Before he left, I promised that I would remain a virgin until he came home. While he was gone we moved to a house in the center of the hood. I finally had my own room and I was excited. At the age of 15, I convinced my mother to allow me to get a job at Popeye's. The manager agreed since I would be turning 16 in a few months. I loved working there. The managers were so understanding and allowed me to work more hours than the other girls because I was able to balance my work school life without complaints.

I didn't mind working on the weekends. For me that meant less time at the house and dealing with all the drama and mess of my step dad and mom. I made up in my mind from the day my mother came and got me from Atlanta that as soon as I could I would work, go to school, keep my grades up and once I graduated that I would enlist in the Air Force and never look back. There was nothing for me in Florida. I didn't feel loved, I didn't feel as if I had the support of my mother. My baby brother and sister were too little to understand what was going on and my brother was just that, a brother. He couldn't understand all that I had gone through or was going through living with my mother.

As I write this, I had a flashback. At this point, I was rebellious, and I was mad at my mother for making me leave Atlanta. I hated living in her house. I felt that I was being looked over and down at now that my mother knew about me almost becoming sexually active. She was on me harder than ever. I've always felt that I was the outcast in my family, I was the darkest and shortest. My family would tease me and say that I was adopted. I didn't have a sense of love or trust for myself.

When I was 13 years old, I was introduced to church. There were some people that would always come to our neighborhood and invite the children to come out. After asking my mother several times, she agreed to let me go. I instantly fell in love with being there. The people there were so nice and welcoming. Every time the doors would open I asked my mother if I could go. It was a small church and it was made up of four families.

I was drawn to working with the youth. After a couple of months, they allowed me to volunteer and work with the babies. It was something about being around the babies that gave me a sense of hope that everything I had gone through would be okay. On the flip side, it made me question my life even more. I didn't like the way I looked. The kids at school were always picking on me, I didn't talk, or dress like them. They would throw things at me and call me names. This behavior made going to school a living hell but being in church made   life   worth   living.

At 13, I confessed my life to Jesus one day in Sunday school. I came home and wrote a note to my mother apologizing to her for everything I had done wrong and that made her disappointed in me and that I wanted our relationship to start over. Note writing was my way of communicating with my mother. I was always felt nervous and couldn't go directly to her and talk about anything. After the incident with my cycle I felt as if I was a disgrace to her and that she didn't love me.

During the summer when I turned 14, the youth department went on a retreat. It was there that I first experienced God's presence and was given the gift of speaking in tongues. I was so excited when I got home, that I shared the news with my mother. It wasn't out of the ordinary for me to come from church and tell my mother what happened, but this time was different. She looked at me as if I was possessed and told me that she didn't want to talk about it. I thought I'd done something wrong. I went up to my room and cried. I was sick of her not understanding me. I was sick of feeling like she didn't love me. I was tired of her and I wanted to run away. I wanted to know where my father was and why I couldn't go live with him again.

Yes, I was looking for love in all the wrong places and it almost got me in trouble once again. This time the guy did the right by leaving and I did right by allowing him to leave. Stay in tune with who your children are communicating with.

We are in an age where they can be texting or on the internet talking to someone across the country who is trying to persuade them to ultimately become a part of a sex trade. Celebrate with your children when significant things that are exciting to them take place. I know that as adults we may be scared as well when we don't understand certain things but be mindful that how you respond to your children is always up to you and can leave an impression that is not so favorable in the child's mind.

As little girls, we dream
our first time being on
our wedding night with
all the bells & whistles
with someone you love
and want to spend the
rest of your life with, but
like many that dream
never turns into a reality.
-unknown

7 NOTING LIKE
THE FIRST TIME

PL was gone, I was in school and working full-time. My focus was keeping my grades up and getting out of my mother's house. It felt as if I was sacrificing being a real teenager. I started to feel lonely and began to desire the "mature" experiences everyone else was having. In our new home I stopped going to church. Without church, I no longer had "big sisters" in my life to hold me accountable. Now the conversations and ideas other girls were talking about intriguing to me. They all stayed out late, drank and smoked. My mom had finally loosened the noose from around my neck, so I had a little freedom.

One day I was working the front register at work and "he" walked in. He was 5'8, caramel skin, honey brown eyes, low haircut, blue jean shorts and a white t-shirt. He was fine! What I remember most about him was thinking it was so funny that his hat was two sizes too big.

"Yo," he said.

Yo? I thought it is official, he was not from around our parts. I snickered.

"What's so funny?" he asked.

"Nothing, just wondering whose attention you are trying to get because I'm standing right here," I said with my sassy attitude.

"Nah shorty, that's how we say hey, hello, you know in Philly."

The thing about my hometown is that there are two Air Force bases located there and there is always a mixture of people rotating in and out of our city. Although I had seen and interacted with my share of guys from working here, there was something different about this dude that attracted me to him.

He and his friend placed their orders and I gave them their drinks.

Take a seat and I'll bring your food out when it comes up."

"Thanks Victoria, I'm looking forward to it," he said as he walked away to find a table.

I'm pretty sure my face looked confused, how did he know my name? I had never seen this guy in my life forgetting I had on my name tag.

As promised when their food came up I walked it over to them. His friend's face was buried in his phone and he appeared to be intrigued by the message.

"Is there anything else I can get for you all?" I asked as I placed their food down.

Before I could walk off Philly reached out and grabbed my hand,

"Can I have your number?"

"No, you cannot and please keep your hands to yourself," I quickly responded.

He and his friend laughed as I walked away. The next 15 minutes were awkward. As they sat there and ate, Philly would look up at the register in attempt to get my attention and I made every effort not to look his way.

Finally, they were done. "Bye Victoria," they both said simultaneously. Although annoying, it made me feel special.

Philly came back a few more times over the next few weeks, this time alone. After the third time, we exchanged numbers and started to talk via e-mail. I let him know that my mom had me on a short leash and that I couldn't go out anywhere. He said he understood and would make sure he saw me on my breaks as much as he could. "I have a friend and maybe sometimes she could bring me to see you," I told him in one of our messages. Tip was my work friend, a couple of years older than me and far more experienced in life. Tip was very tall and thin, and played basketball.

She would take me to see Philly from time to time which eventually led to her talking to his roommate.

One day in May of 2003, my mom was at work and I was told to go to the mall and the movies with my friend Neisha and nothing else. Neisha and I had other plans, we wanted to go hang out with Philly and his friend. He agreed to come and pick us up and take us back to his place. Once we got to his apartment we all watched TV. Neisha was that down for whatever friend, she, "jumped off the porch," way before I did. Girls, guys, whatever, it didn't matter. She was down for whatever with whoever, whenever and if you are wondering yes, she and I had been together sexually as well.

Looking back, I can't remember when she and I started hanging out or when I got so comfortable with her that I never asked her to leave the room. This night, Philly and I were laying in his bed when we started making out. We were heavy on making out and touching, but tonight was different. I had decided this was going to be it. I wanted to go all the way. It wasn't painful, and I didn't cry, but it wasn't magical either. There were no rainbows, gumdrops or lollipops and to my surprise no blood.

As I began to gather myself together Neisha followed me in the bathroom.

"You okay girl?" she asked. I had told her tonight was the night.

"Yeah I'm good." I didn't give her many details.

Philly drove us back to the theatre and he waited in the distance until her mother picked us up. That night I went home, and I cried. I felt as if I had betrayed PL. Part of me wanted to wait on him, but like a can of Pringles, once I popped I couldn't stop. Philly would come and get me on my breaks. We would go behind the strip mall, climb in the back of his black Honda Accord and go at it. As time went by it seemed like that was all he wanted from me.

When Philly and I first started talking he told me about his ex-girlfriend, Moya. He said they had a bad breakup and that she kept trying to get back with him. He never let on that he too wanted to still be with her. I later found out that he didn't mention getting back with her because he never stopped talking to her. She was coming down to visit him quite often. Seeing that my mother wouldn't allow me to date, I was at a disadvantage.

It was a Friday we had gotten to his house and Tip called me.

"Where are you Vic?" When I told her where I was she seemed annoyed?

"I thought you and Philly weren't talking anymore?" "We are just hanging out Tip," no big deal I thought to myself.

"Well I'm not trying to hurt your feelings, but I just wanted you to know that he is still messing with Moya," she went on to say, "Yeah the other day when I was there he was on the phone begging her to come down and see him. He doesn't care about you the way he says he does, he is just using you."

After talking with her I was so angry. I didn't know what to say or what to think. Should I believe her or confront him? I wanted to know so I asked him. Initially he didn't say anything, so I knew it had to be true. He just looked at me in disbelief as if I didn't have a place to speak or question him. I yelled, I threw things around the room and demanded that he answer me.

"You need to leave Victoria," he said angrily.

When I demanded he take me home he refused?

"Since you want to believe everything your friends say then call and tell them to come and get you."

He pushed me out of the door and I sat there for 20 minutes heartbroken, ashamed, embarrassed and confused not knowing what to do. Luckily Tip didn't leave far. I cried the entire way home. I kept telling myself never again will I be a fool for another guy and I meant it. From this moment on I was never going to be in that situation again.

After Philly, I went down a path of destruction. I started talking to guys in the military to see what I could get out of them without catching feelings. I didn't care about anyone's feelings. Why should I? True love was never shown to me. One of my older relatives constantly told me:

"Toy, men are to be used for what they have, take them for what they are worth and have no feelings in it. Life will be much easier."

That became my motto. By the time PL served his 45 days in detention I had five guys under my belt. Wow, I was moving fast.

When PL went to detention, I was a good girl and now I didn't have a care in the world. Something in my heart would not allow me to play with his feelings. Maybe because it was he was the first male that showed me any respect, when I said no to him he listened. Friday, I got a call and it was him telling me that he had gotten out and was coming to see me. Excitement took over my body and I felt like a kid in a candy store. 45 minutes later I spotted him coming up my driveway. 5'11 butterscotch skin and all. My heart was literally in my stomach as he began to walk toward me. "So, what's up?" he asked. I stood there in amazement because it felt as if I had waited a lifetime for him to get out. But, in the same breath I was disgusted with myself. The one thing he had asked of me, to wait on him, I didn't do, and I had to tell him.

As I went inside to get him something to drink I made up in my mind that I had to come clean when I came back.

"It's Meisha's fault," he said, as I told him the story,

"She put you in that situation and she was a bad influence on you, some friend."

He also said that I knew Tip was a known hoe from around the way and I had no business hanging with either of them.

"How could you give yourself to that guy when you barely knew him?" I gave him all the excuses in the world as I sat there so ashamed of myself. We stared at each other for a minute before he said anything else. "It's okay, had I not gotten into trouble you would not have been placed in those situations."

We sat outside chilling for a while before he had to leave to meet up with someone. Knowing where he was going I begged him not to get back into the same mess he was involved in before being locked up.

"I won't," he said.

But we both knew that was a lie.

The next day he picked me up on the corner by my house. Not wanting to hear what anyone had to say I told my family I was going to hang out with some

friends. I was finally being allowed to live a little, but still I knew everyone wouldn't approve of him and the life he chose to live. That night was the first night that he and I went all the way, unlike the rest this was different. It felt different, I felt different and I told myself that this was my first time. I rationalized it by saying this was my first time with someone I cared about and loved. PL cared about me, he always made sure I always had minutes on my phone, he would come and see me on my breaks. He made me happy. Everyone else before him didn't matter anymore. PL and I were good, or so I thought, until one day at work she came to my job claiming to be pregnant by PL. My love, my everything, my PL.

Val hung with this girl named Yo who kept trying to talk to my brother. Every time she called I would hang up the phone. She kept up mess on my job and made my life a living hell. Rumor had it she was loose, and I didn't want my brother around any of that. The previous weekend Tip and I were walking through the mall and as we turned a corner, I spotted her. She and Val stood there looking me up and down. Yo even pointed at me but didn't speak. I rolled my eyes and kept walking. She looked high anyway. She had on a pair of jeans and some red and white Reeboks, but her shirt looked way to small, at least two sizes. As we walked away I could hear them talking and laughing and all I could think was, and she wonders why I don't like her.

The following week at work Val walked in the restaurant where I worked, I was standing at the register and she spoke.

"Toya working?"

"Yeah give me a second, I'll go get her."

I replied. I heard them mumble some things under their breath that I couldn't quite make out.

"I'm hungry, I need to feed my baby!" Val yelled out.

Pregnant I thought to myself, did she just say she was pregnant? I am being who I was you know
curious and all asked. "You're pregnant? I didn't know that."

This time my curiosity got the best of me and I wasn't prepared for her response.

Looking me dead in my eye she said, "Yes I'm pregnant by PL."

My heart dropped, my knees went weak and the room began to spin. I couldn't catch my breath no matter how hard I tried. As I ran to the bathroom I felt my jaws lock and I began to cry.

"The number you have called...," I kept getting his voicemail. Why wasn't he answering? Needing to talk to someone I called my mom. Through the sobs and tears I tried to explain to her what happened.

"PL...she's having his baby...not answering."

Between my broken sentences, she responded, "This is the reason why Victoria, therefore I didn't want you talking to any boys. I'm on my way to get you!"

One thing I knew for sure about mother she would always rescue me if I had a problem.

I couldn't leave the bathroom. I was embarrassed and hurt to say the least.

While I waited on my mother to get there, my manager Meisha came to check on me. She had overheard what the girl said to me.

"I told her that once she got her food she had to leave because she just wanted to start mess."

I was thankful but couldn't respond. Meisha was a cool manager. She was tall, around 5'11, thin frame and wore long thin tracks in her hair. She tried her best to console me and make me feel better about the situation.

"She just wanted to make you upset Vic, don't assume anything she said is true until you talk
to him. Don't let her see you sweat again."

Still crying I asked? "Why would she say that, why? If she has never been alone with him or around him

why would she say that? He has done something with her for her to feel this way and be this confident to come to my job."

At this point my mother walked in and Meisha left us alone to talk. "You need to leave him alone, this is only going to get worse Victoria." Casper said

I didn't want to hear this. I wanted to be reassured that everything would be okay. She asked if I wanted to leave, but not wanting to miss any hours I said no. She left, and I got myself together. I washed my face and reapplied my lip gloss.

Soon as I exited the bathroom, Toya was standing there. I wanted to fight her, but I didn't. I did walk up to her and tell her that I knew she was doing this on purpose.

"You know PL and I talk and you know she was coming up here to try and start some mess with me."

"I didn't know anything about anything, but I do know that PL is not what he makes you believe," she said as she walked away laughing.
Knowing my temper, I walked away.

I called PL all night and he would not answer, he would only text back. Not taking head to what my mom said I took a cab over to his house when I got off. He was shocked when he realized it was me at his door that late. As soon as he opened   the   door,   I

slapped him. As he stood there looking at me in disbelief I started to yell not caring who heard me.

"How could you sleep with her?"

"Calm down," he said, "Come upstairs and let's talk, my mom is asleep."

He sat on his bed with his hands in his head continuously apologizing. No matter how hard I tried, I could not stop the tears from falling.

"Is it true?" I asked hesitantly wanting to know the answer.

"It's a possibility," he whispered. I immediately yelled, "The only way there is a possibility is if you slept with her and without a condom."

His apologies meant nothing. I lost control. Feeling around for the wall I fell back and slid to the grown crying even more.

"Why her?" "What was I doing that was so bad you had to sleep with her. She's not even that cute. Why didn't you use a condom? You don't know if she has anything. She..." He came over to the floor and tried to kiss me,

"I'm sorry baby."

For a moment I started to kiss him back before pushing him off me and slapping him again.

"Take me home," I demanded.

He begged me not to leave and said he wasn't going to take me anywhere until I calmed down and forgave him.

"How do you know it's yours?" I asked still in disbelief. I wanted to know how he was so sure she wasn't sleeping with anyone else.

Not sure what I did to deserve this I asked him again, "Explain to me why you even slept with her?" This time he had a response, "Because you don't do anything, you work and go to school. You don't hang out with us all night and it just happened when we were out smoking one night and..."

I cut him off, "You decided not to wear a condom. You decided that I wasn't good enough. You decided that you don't respect me enough not to sleep with someone else. You decided that you would sleep with a hoe when you have a girlfriend that really loves you and..."

"And she didn't wait on me, she started sleeping with another guy!"

Wow! Did he just say that? I was speechless. I couldn't believe that he was trying to make this about me. This was about the fact that he was out sleeping with someone without a condom.

Using his house phone, I dialed the number for a cab, before I could finish he grabbed the phone and said he would take me home. The 10-minute ride home felt like a lifetime.

A few weeks had passed, and Val wasn't pregnant. She made it all up to get PL to leave me. While we had broken up, we had not stopped talking. My family had moved, and life was looking up. I was happy! However, this was one of three times that PL allegedly had someone else pregnant. Every time was another excuse. Every time I stayed.

Through all the stress of these different females,
I had picked up the habit of smoking Black-n- Mild's. It was something about the smell that calmed my nerves. I would freak that thing just right and Tip and I would pass it back and forth sitting in her car talking about how I needed to leave PL.

The second time he allegedly had a baby on the way, Tip was talking to his best friend. She had overheard Big and PL talking about a girl coming over to his house one night. This Friday night Tip and I got off early. I called PL and let him know we were going to stop by.

"My mom is gone in the car baby, so I can't come get you," he said.

"No worries," I said, "Tip is going to bring me."

That statement was met with silence. Little did he know we had already circled the block and spotted

another car in his yard. Realizing that I was already outside, he accused me of playing games. I knocked on the door and he answered with a beer bottle in his hand. I pushed the door back and noticed there were two females sitting on the couch, not wanting to be rude I spoke and walked directly to the kitchen where I got a knife and placed it in my purse. I walked back in the front room and up the stairs to PL's room. It was then I realized I knew one of the girls, she was a younger girl from around the way. PL followed me upstairs and he closed the door behind him when we got in his room. To his surprise I reached in my purse pulled out the knife and attempted to stab him in his face.

He ducked before the knife hit him and knocked it out my hand. I reached for the bottle that was on the dresser by his door. The bottle hit his head before he threw me on the bed, "Calm your ass down!" he yelled.

I tried to punch him in the face and he pinned me down.

"Calm down, nothing happened," he kept saying. "Your girl Tip is being messy bringing you over here. You need to check her." I got up and reached for the door.

"If nothing happened, then why are they here? I'm going to tell them hoes to leave." He pushed the door shut and pinned me up against the wall. I stared him down in his face and told him I was too young to keep going through this mess with him repeatedly.

"You don't know how to be faithful. I was a fool to think that you would ever grow up." He kept saying he was sorry. "I know," I replied. "You will always be sorry because you are sorry. I am not doing this anymore, I can't." I pushed him off me and ran down the stairs out the door.

Tip had been outside talking to Big this entire time. To me he was just as guilty as PL, so I began to yell at him, "You knew he had a girlfriend, but you didn't try to stop him." Big yelled back at me and told me that's a grown man I can't tell him what to do. As hurtful as it was, he was right.

I didn't speak to PL for weeks after this. I was too hurt. I felt betrayed and I had lost all respect for him. But just like you're probably thinking, we didn't last that long without talking. Eventually PL got himself sent back to detention. This is my time to leave him alone for good I thought to myself.

By this time, I had started working a new job, which is where I met Sal. Sal was an older guy, 27 to be exact and I was only 17. He had come through the drive thru a while ago, but I wasn't interested in talking to him because I was with PL and I didn't want another incident like Philly, but now that PL was gone it was time for me to move on. Sal wasn't like any of the other guys I had dealt with. I know I've said this before, but this time it was true.

He was Asian, short and drove a two door Mitsubishi Galant.

When Sal came along, my mother was very open to him not like all the rest. She told me I should hold on to him and that we would have pretty babies. Again, I was thinking, "Who wants to have a baby?" all I want to do is move far away from this place once I graduate. She never asked, but she was very aware that he was not in high school with me.

Sal was also not like the rest being that he was a lot older. He had a little girl, but I never met her because she lived with her mother and whenever he would have her, I wouldn't be around. Sal introduced me to a life that I fell in love with. He introduced me to how a man was supposed to treat a woman. I never wanted for anything. Whenever we would go shopping there was no limit. Whenever I needed something for school he was just a call away. He never pressured me to do anything with him which made it easier for me to give myself to him, but I could never fully commit to him. I was always looking for him to do something wrong. All the men in my past had only wanted one thing and I couldn't move past this mentality so we fought all the time. I never understood why he wanted to be with a young girl like me. Clearly there were women his own age that he would be happy with, but he would always tell me that I needed to allow love to be easy or I would never truly be happy. I shared with him all that I had been through and he still wanted to be with me.

I was preparing for my senior prom and Sal and I were out looking for dresses. He told me he didn't want to go with me because he didn't want people to look at me weird and judge me for being with an older man. When he first told me I was hurt, but I understood. We were in the dress store when I got a message that PL would be getting out and that he wanted to go to prom with me because he didn't get the opportunity to go to his due to him being in detention. I really wanted to go with him because I still loved him, but I was with Sal now.

Prom came and went, and I thoroughly enjoyed myself. PL had gotten out and Sal and I had a fight of all fights which led to us no longer talking. I was hurt, but I knew I had PL to fall back on. Senior year my schedule was open during the end of the day and I would spend that part of the day with PL. I thought this time was going to be different. He had been gone for a while and I prayed that his time he would come back a different guy and we would live happily ever after. I will admit that it did start off that way, but in a matter of weeks, he was back to his old ways.

After only two months of being out, there was another female claiming to be pregnant by him.

She was close to her due date. I was so pissed. Not only was he messing with another female before he went to detention, this one was about to have a baby. One night I went over to his house and his mother tried to come in his room, but he had the door locked. She was pissed because she wanted the house phone, so she started yelling

"PL I am sick of you having these fast ass little girls in my house. Tell her she has to go."

I was pissed, I looked over at him

"Who else have you been bringing here PL? Are you that disrespectful that you sleep with them where you slept with me?"

I waited until I thought his mom was in the bed and I called a cab. While I was waiting, he kept trying to explain that she didn't know anything. I sat there in complete silence. I realized that he was a complete liar and that he was never going to change. I also realized that I was a liar and that I was lying to myself thinking we were ever going to work out.

That night when I got home I made up in my mind that I was done, and I needed to get as far away from him as possible because he was never going to change. As long we were in the same city, I was going to keep coming back to him. I was committed to going to the Air Force and nothing was going to stop me. This city had nothing else to give me. My mother's dad was an athletic director at a college in Alabama and offered me a chance to come to school there. For the first time, the Air Force was now a second option.

I started a new job at Wal-Mart and started saving money and putting layaways up to make sure I had everything I needed for school. I was all set or, so I thought. My little brother's dad had lost his job and now my mother was demanding I start helping with the bills. I remember laying on the couch in my brother's room when she walked in and said,

"Victoria, I need you to give me some money on the bills," at first, I ignored her because I thought clearly, she was having a moment. How could she want me to pay any bills with a man living here with us, so I kept playing on my phone?

She came in the room and stood in

front of me, "Do you hear me?"

I sat up.

"Why do I have to give you any money?"

I could tell that she was getting pissed off.

"Because you live in my house, you eat my food, so I think you need to give me something on these bills."

Realizing that she was serious I was pissed as hell by now.

"You have a man living here and I am a child, why do I need to help you pay bills? I don't have to pay any bills, make him get a job and help you."

She started cussing and I started fussing

back.

"Since you think you're grown," she growled "you can get the fuck out of my house." I didn't even reply I just called my friend Bre.

Bre was 20 with two little girls of her own and she was always telling me that I should leave my mother's house because she treated me like a little girl.

"You have no freedom there," she would say.

By now I had called a cab. My mom was in her room cursing about how terrible and grown I thought I was. When the cab pulled up, my step dad begged me not to leave. All I could think is why was he talking to me, I do not like him, and he knows it. He always said and did inappropriate things toward me. He was always cheating on my mom and to me he was trash. How dare he try to come save me when their entire relationship was built on a lie? I shut the door in his face and told the driver where to take me.

I cried the entire way to Bre's house. How could a mother choose a man over her own child? What had I done that made my mother hate me so much? I vowed that day I would never have any children because I didn't want to end up like her or worse.

I was at Bre's house an entire month before my mom called and asked me to come home. At first, I hesitated to go back, but Bre's house was no better. She had men running in and out and her daughters were bad as hell. She didn't keep a clean house and I didn't understand how men even dealt with her when she was so nasty. That was when I realized that my mom was right when she said, "Men will sleep with anything in the dark as long as they can get off."

By now I had decided that college was for me, I only needed to make it three more months at my mom's house. I promised myself that once I left I would never come back here, no matter what life threw at me and until this day I have never returned home.

I know this was long and drawn out, but I really want people to understand that sex is more than an orgasm and a thing to do. It is more than a fairytale wedding day that takes place with, "Mr. who we think is right." Speaking for myself, I was looking for something and it seemed as if I found it when I met PL, but that was a smokescreen. Yes, he respected me enough not to keep going when I said stop, but that was it. I was still young impressionable, looking for love, comfort, safety and security in a boyfriend and most importantly I was vulnerable and PL new that it took it for what it was worth.

Of course, it would have been great for him to come home and have sex with a virgin. It probably gave him something to look forward to during his 45 day stay in detention, but to my point neither one of us knew what real love was. Sex was only part of the equation. Philly was the first man that I let my guard down with and he seemed to know that I didn't know any better. He would often tell me that my mother had me on a short leash and he wanted to do more with me than see me on my lunch breaks. However, this was a ploy to make me feel as if he really cared. All the while he was sleeping with his ex and other females that I went to school with. This however wasn't discovered until years later when he and I had a conversation and he apologized for ever hurting me. Not to mention that I was only 16 and he was 20 and by law I wasn't old enough to consent to sex and had my mother known, she could have pressed charges for rape. Emotions, expectations, trust, loyalty, and a whole host of other things come with a relationship. Be mindful of this and be smart enough to know when you have set yourself up for failure and you are being stringed along. Maturity comes through experiences that have been well learned, not from age.

So, you left the situation now you must start over. You must live your life like you have it all together because you're afraid of being judge!
-Victoria Necole

8 THE NEW ME

Man, oh man! What was this newfound life!? Freedom! I could do whatever I wanted to do. This was something that I wasn't accustomed to. There were people from all over in one place and I felt like a little girl in a candy shop. This was my time to reinvent myself, I knew no one here and no one knew me. However, with my grandad working for the college I knew everything that I did had to be done without a trace.

It was homecoming weekend and I was sitting in my Pa's office when some guys walked in wearing gold boots and purple jackets.

"Why would someone paint their shoes that color?" I asked my Pa.

He laughed, "They're in a fraternity that's why. Did you have any sororities or fraternities at your school back home?"

I had never heard the word fraternity or sorority, but I was determined to find out all about these guys. When I got back to my room, my roommate, who was more experienced with talking to boys, told me that she wanted to go to a house party someone was having that weekend.

"How did you meet these guys?" I asked.

She must have sensed my hesitancy.

"Chill, we are going to be okay, it will be fun."

Later that evening two guys called our room phone and told us to come downstairs. The two guys were very polite, I thought to myself that I had seen them before and I think they played football. Yes, that was it they had come up to me earlier that day when I was speaking to my Pa on the field.

When we arrived at the house party we were the only ones there. Some party I thought to myself.

"Yall want something to drink?" they offered from the kitchen.

Not knowing them I knew I did not want anything mixed, plus I had never really had a drink before.

"I'll start with a cooler," I replied.

By this time, more people were arriving. I had found my way to the card table and they were pumping me up to have some shots.

"Nah, but I'll have that other drink you all were mixing up."

Surprisingly it was good, "This tastes like Kool-Aid." I mentioned to one of them and before I knew it I had drank two glasses.

"Slow down baby girl," one of them said.

Not liking being told what to do I instructed them to mind their business and stood up to go the bathroom. Immediately I hit the floor.

Everyone was laughing,

"Hey, take her outside to get
some air before she passes out."

I heard one of them say. We were already close to the door so luckily, I didn't have far to walk. As I sat outside on the ground playing in rocks
someone walked up,

"Is that coach's granddaughter? Someone gets her out of here before she gets us all in trouble."

Next thing I know I was being picked up and laid in a bed in the back room. Big mistake, as soon as he laid me down I began throwing up from my mouth and my nose, I was choking. My roommate tried to help me to the bathroom, but every time I stood up I would fall. Once I even hit my head and apparently passed out. When I woke up everyone had left to go to the step show. I was embarrassed, and my roommate was pissed. We had no way back to the yard and when the guys returned home they were too drunk to drive us, so we had to stay the night.

That following morning Donnie came in the room.

"Hey, do you know what happened last night?"

I shook my head no and he began to tell me everything that had taken place the night before. I was so ashamed. How could I allow myself to get into a situation like that? All I remember saying was please don't tell my Pa.

He agreed.

"You know if it had been anyone else they may have taken advantage of you and you would not have known," he said.

I respected him so much for that reality check. From that point on, he and I became close. But, eventually we slept together and the whole situation was terrible.

"This is garbage, we really need to stop," I said to him in the middle of us having sex.

He looked at me as if I was crazy was crazy. "What, are you sure?"

"Yes" I replied with an attitude, "You should be ashamed of yourself. You call yourself a nasty dog and you can't even keep me entertained."

His breath reeked of alcohol and I felt he needed to think of how he was lacking as a man before he ruined another night with another female. The look he gave me as he sat up was as if he wanted to slap fire from my mouth. At this time his phone rang, and it was his mother.

"I got company Ma. I really like her, but she hurt my feelings," then he handed me the phone. "Hello," I answered, she asked me why I was being mean to her son. I don't think she was prepared for what came next. Attitude in place.

I replied, "Ma'am would you want me to lie to your son and have him thinking that what he is doing is pleasing to me or other women?" there was a moment of silence followed by a, "no."

"Great," I told her, "That is why I didn't lie to him, he needs to do better!" and I handed him back the phone. When he was done talking to her I asked if he could take me back to the yard. He and I didn't talk much after that. I had found my edge- I was never going to get close to another guy and give him all of me before he hurt me I was going to hurt him.

The semester was almost over, and we were out for the Thanksgiving holidays. I went home and visited PL when I was there. Word on the street was the last jump-off had had her child. Must have been true because as I opened the door to his room I was paralyzed in the doorway with tears rolling down my face. He had baby clothes and diapers lined up against the wall. There was a playpen and a bassinet in the corner of the room. He reached for my hand.

"I'm sorry Vic, but I can't abandon my child."

There had been no DNA test to confirm it was his, but because there was even a possibility he didn't want to regret not being there and doing for the baby. Truth is I admired him for this, but the hurt wasn't any less. I knew I had to stick to my decision of leaving this city. That was my last night there, I never returned to see him.

Would you keep your hand on burning fire?

-Victoria Necole

9 MR. WRONG

To be honest I am not sure how he and I officially started talking. Initially his friend was using his profile to communicate with me and I found out that the guy I was talking to was not who I thought it was, but nevertheless Mr. Wrong and I started hanging out on campus. Wait! Let me start off by saying caramel and vanilla were never really my favorite type of ice cream, but for him I gave it a try.

I remember the first time we met, we were in the cafe. He had on red basketball shorts, a white tee and a pair of Nike flip flops. Looking back, I should have never entertained him wearing flip flops and socks, that isn't normal. Nevertheless, he approached me and spoke. He explained how he allowed his friend to use his messenger, but he really wanted to talk to me, not his friend. I was so taken aback and confused. What was this game they were trying to pull? My first impression of him was a lie and I wasn't sure if I wanted to talk to him because surely that wasn't a good way to start a relationship.

He looked shocked, he couldn't believe I was rejecting him. Back then I loved to play hard to get although in my head I had already slept with him and his little friend. Truth is, I still wanted to talk to him, but I didn't want him to think that just because he apologized to me I was going to be hanging on to every word he said. We went our separate ways but continued to message each other throughout the day. Later, that night I decided to meet him on the yard in front of the science building. It was toward the end of the year and most kids had started going home, perfect because privacy was key for me. I was not a fan of everyone knowing everything I was doing so this was the perfect time for us to hang out.

One thing I liked about Mr. Wrong was that he was very apologetic. Whenever he felt as if he had hurt my feelings or made me feel anyway other than happy. He was right there working to bring a smile back to my face from day one. That night as I sat on his lap wearing my white terry cloth romper we discussed our plans for the summer. I had planned to go back east to visit my family and he was upset that I wouldn't be around.

"I don't have a need to stay here in town," I reminded him.

"I should be taking classes, but I'm not really feeling it."

He seemed even more upset when I told him I wouldn't be coming back to the HBCU. "It's not personal, this has been a big eye opener for me and what I'm used to. It's vastly different from all the schools I've gone to my entire life."

I was thankful for my time there and the experience that it showed me I could never get back, but the time had come for us to part ways. He looked at me so confused.

"This isn't my first-choice school, but I do have an athletic scholarship so I'm here."

He explained to me that he and his family weren't big on him getting loans and didn't want to spend the rest of his adulthood paying them back. I respected his choices.

Our lives were so different, he was raised with his mother and father. His mom was a real-estate agent and his dad did something with athletics. Whenever we would discuss my father not being in my life, he would look at me as if I was speaking a foreign language. Over the summer, Mr. Wrong and I would talk every blue moon. His inconsistency caused me to feel uneasy. He had a sneakiness about him and I questioned if I was good enough for him.

During the summer I had some much-needed fun. I went to clubs in DC with my family. They were nothing like I expected and even though I couldn't drink, my family made sure I had plenty of fun. I was 19 and I was living the life. My family managed to get me a job at the commissary on base as a secretary to the store manager's secretary. My job consisted of tons of paperwork, mainly filing and answering the phones. Most days I stayed in my office reading books. This was how I discovered Zane. Her writing made me feel I could live an entirely different life and no one would ever find out, and slowly but surely, I did.

Being around older women, I would hear them talk about a website called *Black Planet* and my interest was piqued so I joined. I know, I know why was someone my age thinking about a dating website? By this point it is no secret that I was promiscuous. I had been with well over 10 guys since losing my virginity.

Instantly I came across a profile of a guy that caused my mouth to drop. He was 23 years old, 6'2, braids to the back and light pink lips. I thought I had died and gone to Heaven. I sent him a message and he responded rather quickly. He asked me for my number and he called me later that night. I don't remember talking to anyone else.

We laughed and talked for hours.
He joked about how I talked

"I am not from up here, this is only my 2nd time here."

I let him know I was there for the summer and would be leaving in a month and a half.

"Can I take you out this weekend?" he offered.

He must be psycho I thought to myself. He doesn't even know me and wants to take me out. By now you may think I was savage back then, but, I was all bark and no bite.

Talking on the phone was all good, but I wasn't sure if I wanted to meet him. I spoke with my family about it and they agreed he could come over first before they allowed me to go out with him.

He came over Friday after work with flowers and a pack of twizzles, he smelled good enough to lick. His pictures did him no justice, this man was handsome! This was the beginning of my relationship with Idaguy. Since I knew I was going back to school soon I assumed this was nothing more than a summer fling. Every weekend we went all over the DMV. Something about dating an older man was a total turn on, my attraction to him made it easy to sleep with him. There were times my guilt got the best of me because I knew I was still talking to Mr. Wrong and there was a better chance he and I would end up together. During our conversations, I told Ida guy all about Mr. Wrong and surprisingly he was cool about everything.

That fall I transferred to U of A. Looking back I should have left Mr. Wrong during that transition because it became an out of sight, out of mind situation. "The Book" was just getting hot and only college students could use it. Mr. Wrong began to use it for his flings. I would go on his page and see comments from girls like, "It was nice to see you," or, "We should hang out again soon." I would question him, and his response was "I didn't have a choice, but to be around them, they were over my homeboy's house and I couldn't be rude." Not holding him accountable I began to dislike his boys.

Everything he did wrong was his boy's fault.

Reflecting, I had no right to be upset with them. Mr. Wrong like PL was an adult and it wasn't their fault he couldn't keep his hands, feet and other objects to himself. Truth is I couldn't hold them accountable because I had never held the first man in my life, my father, accountable.

Spring 2007 was one of the hardest times of my life. One of my closest friends was sentenced to a little under a year for doing something that they had no business doing. Yes, they were guilty, but we were so close, and it hurt. I will never forget I got the call while sitting in class. I went into the hallway and as soon as I was informed what was going on, I had to lean against the wall to catch my balance. I don't know how long I stood there staring out of the window not understanding why bad things happen to people with a good heart.

That night Mr. Wrong came over my apartment. I didn't really want company, but I wanted someone that I thought loved me to be around. He didn't understand why I wanted to lay in the room with the lights off and cry.

"Please don't talk," I asked him, "just hold me." He kept complaining

"If you don't want to talk about it I can get J to pick me up and take me back to the yard."

I couldn't believe how selfish he was being. I knew about the girl in the band he had been kicking it with on the yard and a part of me didn't want him to go because I kept thinking he just wanted to go be with her. I was hurt and scared, I was disappointed in him, but I was going to   show   him.

"You can you come and pick me up,"

I heard him on the phone with his friend. I gathered myself put my pants on and grabbed my purse and keys,

"Hang up the phone, I'll take you back."

The 7-minute drive back to his yard was cold and silent. We pulled in the parking lot and I didn't even put the car in park. As he leaned over to say goodbye and kiss me, I leaned away and nodded. He had one foot outside the car and I started to reverse.

"Don't you ever call me again!" I yelled out the door.

For a split second, I felt bad. The door hit his leg and he stumbled. What if he had gone under the car? What if he had really gotten hurt? I didn't care, he had hurt me. For so long he had been cheating on me and now when I needed him the most he made my hurt all about him.

The nerve of him.

We played the on again off again game for a few weeks. I had no idea why I was giving this boy another chance.? He was no different than PL. He was the same person in another body in a different city. What was the issue in my life? Was it me or was it them? I had just come back from visiting Idaguy and I was on cloud 9, but I decided to give Mr. Wrong one last chance. Soon as I arrived back in town, the drama was waiting on me at the door.

A few weeks had passed, and we were off and on yet again. Why was I giving this man another chance? He was no different from PL just a different guy, different face from another city.

My roommates and I were hanging out in our apartment talking when his name came up. They asked what was going on with us and I told them that we were on again and off again. I wanted to know what they had to say so I didn't tell them he was coming over that night.

"I was around the corner at another girl's house when his name came up," Britany said, "Turns out he is sleeping with her roommate."

Immediately I pulled her up on the book and became pissed, "She is not even cute." How could he be with someone that wasn't as cute as I was? I began to yell.

Side note: Why do females always think it's all about the looks? You think I would have learned by now after dealing with PL.

I texted him to come over earlier, but he didn't respond. My rage grew, "I don't care if you don't answer the phone I am coming to find you," I texted him. He knew causing a scene was nothing to me. I called him again and he answered. "Are you meeting with another girl?" He got defensive and told me that listening to Britany wasn't the right thing for me to do. I knew then that everything she said to me was true and he had to see me about this. Yes, I had been doing my mess, but I was still hurt, and I felt played. My mess was never close to home I made sure of that.

My roommates tried to calm me down, but I was getting even more upset. I was calling him back and texting him and he wouldn't respond. I wanted to fight now! I left the house and headed towards where I knew he would be.

I stood outside his friend's house as I noticed J's truck pass me and Mr. Wrong was in the passenger seat. They went around the corner then the truck came back. This time no one was in the passenger seat. I walked up to J, "Do NOT get in the middle of this J, this is your fault," I yelled at him, "Every time a new girl pops up you are in the middle of it. Hell 9 out of 10 times they are smashing at your house."

He looked dumbfounded, "I don't know what you're talking about, Mr. Wrong isn't here."

"I don't know what game Yall are trying to play," I said as I walked closer and closer to him, "but you better call your boy because I am about to key his car up." By this time, I was walking towards his car, I got close enough and stuck my key in the passenger door. Not 5 seconds later Mr. Wrong came running from behind the building. I had made myself comfortable on the trunk where I was drawing circles.

"Please stop baby, stop," he begged.

When he got close enough I slapped him and grabbed his lanyard pulling him towards me and wrapped it around my hand,

"Don't lie to me, have you been sleeping with the fat b***h that lives around the corner from my apartment?"

"No," he said quickly.

I gripped the lanyard tighter.

"Please stop," he gasped, "Let go. I chilled with her twice, but we never slept together. She asked me to come listen to her sing and said she wanted to give me a massage."

Tears started forming in my eyes. How could I be mad at him? I wasn't here, and we were on another break. I hugged him and gave him a kiss. As we begin to walk toward J's house a car pulled up and parked right in the middle of the road. It was "her."

She got out, "How could you do this to me?" she yelled at him. "I told you I didn't want to be in any mess or drama and you said you would never hurt me."

Shocked, I dropped his hand and stepped back.

He walked toward her, "Calm down,"

What was going on? I was speechless standing there looking at him trying to calm her down.
By now tears were flowing down my cheeks.

"Did he tell you he wanted to date you?" I asked her.

"Yes" she replied. I looked at both

"Yall can have each other."

I got in my car and drove off. As I passed them, he was now leaning on J's truck talking to her. I rolled down my window and yelled out

"I wish all the best of luck in yall's relationship."

I went home and cried until I couldn't cry anymore. I was sick of being mistreated. I wanted a real relationship that was healthy and trusting.

That night I prayed:

"God please send me someone that will love me, someone that has the same faith as me. Someone who treated me nice and everyone wanted. Someone who loved me unconditionally. And someone who would be honest about the girls he is with."

Never in a million years did I think that I would get exactly what I wanted in just a few weeks never did I think I had just spoken a curse over my life.

Stop playing with your past if you want your future to be different!

-Victoria Necole

10 SECURE THE BAG

What do you do when all you know
is how to "get it?"

When people constantly say, "Girl you
should never go broke with what you
have between your legs," as if that's the
only asset I or any woman has.

For as long as I can remember, these
words have played over and over in my
mind throughout various situations in my
life. Developing before the rest of the
girls in my class always made me eye
candy to the little boys in school. They
didn't necessarily like me or want to date
me, but they knew what they wanted to
do to me.

During college, I attempted to reinvent
myself. No longer was I the girl in the
shadows of the hallways wishing I could
sit with the "cool kids." I was going to be
a cool kid, I could do whatever I wanted
here. No one could question me about my
past because no one here knew me.

I had no real plans to move and be with
Idaguy, I enjoyed talking to him and we

eventually became great friends. He kept money in my pocket and knew how to lift my spirits when things got rough, but it wasn't enough. Before transferring schools, I linked up with some older girls who were into getting money on another level. They introduced me to an older white man who owned his own car dealership.

"All you have to do is have a couple of conversations with him and he will help you get a car," Ten said.

I was nervous, but what harm would be having conversations do? I was 21 and although I didn't have my driver's license I did need a car of my own. Ten and I went to the dealership to talk to Stan. He was short with salt and pepper hair, he was wearing cargo shorts and his company polo. Like most people in town, he had U of A football pictures everywhere. His entire conversation was centered on how he went there years ago and how athletic he was. He gave me a few compliments about my body and even tried to touch me. I felt so uncomfortable, but I wanted a car, so I stayed.

Several weeks later, Stan was calling and texting me daily. I had gotten my car, so I continued the charade. He kept trying to persuade me to come over, so he could cook for me and give me money for my car note. Everything in me told me not to go, but my current job wasn't paying me much and I had run through my refund check from school, so I was desperate. His house was cleaner than I expected, what I wasn't surprised by was the U of A paraphernalia that lined the freshly remodeled basement. I could smell the grill going. We sat at the table talking about Ten for a while before going in the living room. Immediately upon entering the living room I noticed porn playing on the television. I knew then I had made a mistake and should get up and leave, but my curiosity got the best of me.

How far was he going to try and go with me?

"Do you want to come in my room?" he asked. I was scared, but I went.

"I don't want to have sex with you, I know that's what you're thinking."

Slightly relieved I wasn't ready for what he did want.

"I just want to watch you masturbate with this toy," he said as he pointed to the toy already laid out on the bed.

Immediately I began to wonder why in the world he had this toy and am I the only one who he has asked to do this.

"I'll pay you $400 if you do it," he interrupted my thoughts.

Without a second thought I did it. I was already sleeping with guys and only getting hurt from their mistrust and lack of loyalty so why not get paid for it.

As I lay there on the bed masturbating with the toy he stood beside the bed touching himself. All I could think was hurry up and get this over with. I wish I could say this was the only time this happened, but it went on for several months. I was going at least twice a week collecting $300-$500 each time. There were even times I didn't have to sleep with him. I could pull up to his mailbox and pick up a package. After a couple of months, I realized I wasn't the only one he was sleeping with. I had been in denial thinking I was the only one, thinking he cared about me. Dumb, I know. I was still looking for love in all the wrong beds.

Even though I needed the money, I was tired, I became greedy, this had become a drug to me. I needed more money faster and I didn't want to deal with the times he would deny me. He seemed to be pulling back from me, but I was used to the money by now and had to find a way to continue getting it plus more. Plus, I was tired of laying on my back with him, he disgusted me. This crap had to come to an end.

My friend Niece was my go to girl, she was like Neisha from back in the day. Down for anything so I knew she would be down for making some coins. I told her about Stan and how he wasn't something to run home about but it was a nice business. I showed her how she and I could make a quick $1000 dealing with him. What I didn't tell her is that Stan was going to pay me extra for every girl I brought him.

Yes, you can officially say that I prostituted and pimped other women out. I was living life in the fast lane going nowhere quick! Once again sex became a way of getting things I wanted. Sex became my meal ticket and a way out of no way. The lack of money and knowing that men would pay decent money for sex didn't make my decisions difficult. Parents, aunts, friends, neighbors and strangers who care, understand this, when children especially your daughters are in situations where they need money. You subliminally teach them to be a whore by saying things such as, "You should never go broke with what's between your legs," and that mindset opens doors that only God can close.

Even if that's the way you were treated or the way you lived, at the end of the day this should be the last thing that you want for your children. Be there, listen, and continue to help as much as you can. Teach them their value and that what is between our legs is sacred and worth preserving.

Older teens, 15 to 16-year-olds, are more likely to say teens having oral sex are still virgins than are 13 to 14- year-olds (60% vs. 46%).

Suburban teens (60%) are more likely to say teens who have oral sex are still virgins than teens who live in an urban environment (45%).

11 MR. P.O.B.

Insert Getting people to do things for me has never been an issue so Mr. P.O.B was no different. Nautica, new friend, and I had been to the P.O.B several times, but this night was different. We skipped to the front of the line like always, got patted down and paid the fee. Straight to the bathroom we went. We came out of the bathroom and snapped a couple of pictures then headed to the bar. We located our favorite bartender, the white girl, she was the best bartender in the club plus she always gave us a little more alcohol in our drinks.

Never really wanting anyone to know how much I drank not wanting to come off as the drunk girl in the club who couldn't hold her liquor I came up with a plan, or so I thought. I would order three Amaretto Sours. Take two to the head and walk around sipping the last one. Looking back, I am laughing because I didn't really hide it well at all. I would become an emotional drunk.

I was under the influence of at least four drinks when we met, so how we met is fuzzy. "If you are going to stare you could at least buy us a drink," I remember shouting down the bar after noticing that he was staring at us.

"What did you just say to me Black?" who the hell was he talking to I thought to myself.

"First my name is Victoria. Second, if you're going to stare the least you can do is buy me and my girl a drink."

We just stood there staring at each other for what felt like forever

"I'll do it as long as you give me your phone number,"

I laughed and gave it to him but gave him the disclaimer that I couldn't promise anything would come from it.

I've regretted a lot of things in my life and this night I regretted accepting his $8 drink, he became my shadow that night. That drink turned into what felt like a lifetime commitment. He was on my heels the entire night. We tried to get away from him by going to the bathroom but when we came out he and his friend were standing outside the door waiting on us.

"Did I miss something by accepting this drink?" I finally asked

"Do you feel like I owe you something because if so let me go and give you these $8 back."

At this point I was reaching in my purse, I would pay anything to get him off me.

"You are one sexy mother*****, can we all hang out after we leave here?"

Hang out? I was trying to get rid of him.

"I'm not single," I said to him, "and I have no intentions of doing anything with you or your friend after the club at 3 am. What kind of female do you think I am?"

He continued to press me, "Man Black, I wasn't trying to come at you like that. I just wanted to kick it with you."

I rolled my eyes and reminded him that whatever type of female he was used to picking up I was not her and she was not me. Because my friend and I were bi-weekly visitors, I saw him on our next go round. Of course, my current, unreliable, always cheating boyfriend and I were on another breakup so I entertained Mr. POB a little more this time. We continued to meet up bi-weekly. It wasn't unusual for us to argue at the club as if we were a married couple although we had known each other less than a month.

When I drank my emotions were high and when I went out I was always feeling myself. Mr. POB was hood, but he also had a gentlemen side to him. Whenever we left the club he would always make sure we made it to our car safely, we normally parked in the alley. On this night Nautica ran into an old friend of hers who met us at our car. As they engaged in conversation, Mr. P.O.B. offered to perform oral sex on me.

"You don't know me from Keisha or Ebony," I replied.

"I'm not trying to get any, I just want to see if you taste as good as you look," he said with a smirk on his face.

A little back history about me. I wasn't as innocent as people thought I was, or at least as I thought I was. I wasn't known on the yard, but I did my dirt and I like to think I was very good at hiding it. I dared dudes to put my business in the street. Reality is I wasn't going to do anything if they did, I couldn't do anything. I don't know if the guys did talk, but what I do know is that it never got back to me. That's where I like to think that God's grace and mercy kept me even when I didn't keep myself.

After a long deep stare and questioning myself we climbed into the back of my car and he did just that. Not once did he ask me to touch him or ask for anything in return. At one point my friends guy friend obviously saw something because I heard my friend say stop staring, but I didn't care. I was at a point in my life where internally I was very depressed. I was tired of being cheated on and I wanted to feel loved. For the moment Mr. POB filled that void. After he did his business, he got out the car and grabbed for his stuff on top of the car, had a drink and told us to drive home safely.

This was so wild for me, but what do you do when you are broken and looking for love in all the wrong places? When you don't know who you are or whose you are. When you think love is giving a piece of you to anyone who tells you that you are beautiful, this is exactly the type of road you can end up on.

When I look back on my behavior my whole life style starting with the molestation at seven framed my thoughts and behavior in a sexual way. Sometimes we are quick to judge and criticize people, especially women, who have had a less than perfect lifestyle not knowing the foundation of how their world was framed from the beginning. I urge to seek the best in people even when you are aware of the worse.

What you spoke yesterday has become your today's reality. So, what do you speak today that will change your tomorrow?
-Victoria Necole

12 MR. WRONG - TOO

I can honestly say that this was my fault, I have no one to blame for these actions, but myself. I remember it very well. This was the last weekend for a while that I would be able to go to the POB. I was starting a new job. It was June of 2008 and my friend, Nautica had recently met someone while working at the local retail store. She couldn't wait for me to meet him, you know how friends are.

"Girl I want you to meet this guy," she would say, "First I want to see if you know him and second see if you get a weird vibe from him."

Nautica had been outside talking to him for a few minutes before she called and told me to come down.

"I'm in the middle of cutting my hair," I told her.

She didn't care, "Girl if you don't leave your hair alone before you mess something up, come down here really quick."

Ignoring her comment about my hair, I cut it, now I had a new full forehead bang. I peeped out the window and I noticed a second guy standing there. She better not be trying to hook me up I thought. Mr. Wrong and I are on another break, but I'm not sure I want to move on and talk to anyone else. She called me again. I knew I had to hurry or we risked not getting to the club on time.

My stomach began to turn as I walked down the stairs. When I got to the bottom, Mr. Wrong- Too was standing there is his khaki shorts and polo inspire shirt. I stood there with looking at him. There was something about him that caused me to become speechless. We all shared an awkward moment of silence. Nautica went on to introduce me to her dude and he in returned introduced me to Mr. Wrong-too He stated his name and I told him mine.

"I know you getting ready to go out," he said, "But can I have your number?"

Looking him dead in the eye I said, "You're a little boy and nothing good will ever come from you."

Nautica looked at me in disbelief and I turned and began walking back up the stairs.

"I'm not a little boy," Mr. Wrong-too said, he had followed me and was right on my heels,

"I'm a grown man and I take care of my own."

Now at the top of the stairs I turned around. As I walked in my room he was still following me. I ignored him and began to work on my hair.

"Didn't your mother ever tell you it was rude to stare?" I said as I glanced in the mirror and noticed him staring at my butt.

He laughed. "If you give me your number I wouldn't have to stare, and we could talk when you got home."

I politely walked over to him, grabbed his hand and escorted him to the door. Later that night my friend and I went out which of course meant I was linking up with POB.

Mr. Wrong and I still communicated from time to time, but I was too busy to give him a lot of my energy. I was working, going to class and trying to *secure the bag* whenever I could. A few days had passed and one day while bored at work, I texted Nautica to ask her friend if she could ask her friend for the little boy's number that came by the house the other night. She told me I was crazy and that he wouldn't want my number after my being mean to him. A few moments had passed, and she replied with his number.

I texted and asked him what he was doing.

He replied saying, "I am glad you had a change of heart because I really want to get to know you."

"I'm at work, but you should bring me some grapes and let's talk about this cocky attitude you have."

Two hours later he showed up at my job. He asked me why was I giving him such a hard time the other night as he sat on the wall beside the building? I explained to him that he had a cocky attitude and that he seemed like the type of guy that was used to getting what he wanted from females.

He stared with disbelief, he replied, "Ma I'm not cocky this is just who am!"

There was something about this man that my flesh wanted to know more about all the while my mind was telling me that I was about to make the biggest mistake of my life.

My flesh won, and I invited him over that night. "How many girls are you talking to?" I asked as he sat on my bed. I needed to know what I was getting into. "10," he replied.

"Ok and how many are you sleeping with?"

"3, but I'm not in a committed relationship with anyone."

Right then I should have left him alone. But in my mind, I romanticized what he had told me. I felt it was a breath of fresh air to have someone be honest and upfront with me. We had sex that night, but something strange happened. *I died.* I know what you are thinking, but I remember while we were being intimate I looked up at the mirror that was on the back of my door and I could hardly see my reflection. Something came over me and I felt like I made the worst decision, the biggest mistake of my life. Two days later I became very ill, so I went to the student health center.

"I'm sorry Ms. Long, but you have a virus."

The doctor's words stung. I was so upset; how could this happen to me. Did I really expect anything other than this? I slept with a man I hardly knew with no condom. I kept telling myself my life was over. Trying to get my mind off it I went to work, but I couldn't focus so I left. I couldn't understand how I could allow this to happen to me I'm health major all I do is study the effects of sexually transmitted diseases. I was disappointed in myself. I felt as if I let the entire world down. I called my friend Nautica.

Nautica called Mr. Wrong-Too and tried to explain to him what was going on. For some reason after that I felt as if I was stuck with him. We tried to work things out and create a solid relationship, but he was never committed to me. We had only been dating a few weeks when a female called my phone. The one whose honesty I admired, failed to mention he had a baby back home by someone who was petty and immature. The mother of his child found out where I worked as a sitter and applied to work there. She even told Mr. Wrong-too that I was cheating on him with a coworker.

It was normal for me to go to his house and see condom wrappers on the floor.

"Those are someone else's," he would always say.

With no proof, I had no choice but to believe him. We swept it under the rug and had sex. I was an advocate for not questioning anyone unless you have solid proof. I had no idea how to have an adult conversation about things. I literally felt as if I was under a spell. I would always tell him that one day I would wake up from this nightmare, that the girl he was cheating on me with would be who he ended up with. He would get so upset.

"We are never going to break up Victoria, you are stuck with me for the rest of your life."

I knew this was not the life God had for me. This could not be what *real* love was. How could this be what I must live for after praying to God about what I wanted?

There was never peace in our relationship. We would break up weekly which resulted me going back to Mr. Wrong and him going back to his ex. This cycle was never ending until May of 2008 when I ended up in the hospital.

Earlier that day he had my car while I was in class. He picked me up and we grabbed something to eat before heading back to my place. After becoming intimate, I took a nap before having to go to work. I woke up to him on my computer, I didn't think anything about it was normal due to his job. It didn't seem unusual until I tried to kiss him, and he didn't speak to me or say anything. Unsure of what was going on I went to take a shower. On the way to work I kept asking what was wrong, "Leave it alone," he would say.

Not able to focus at work I kept texting him trying to talk to him, he would wait several minutes before texting back.

"If you don't talk to me about it, then just   bring me my car."

I texted him. He responded, "That's not what you want."

By this time, I was getting frustrated, so I demanded he bring me my car. After about 2.5 hours he text and told me he was outside. When I walked outside he was leaning up against my car with his hands folded.

"Can I have my keys please?" I asked.

"Do you have something to tell me?" he questioned.

"Um, no" I replied. When I looked at him his eyes   were dark black.

"You're a liar. I saw a message from Mr. Wrong and you wishing him success and you love him and shit. Then I saw another message where you were reminiscing and whatever."

Surprised that he had gone through my stuff, I asked him if he had read the messages in their entirety.

"The messages with Mr. Wrong were innocent and with the other guy you would have saw where
I told him to stop because I had a boyfriend."

At that moment it felt as if everything stopped. He grabbed me by my throat and slammed me up against my car. I passed out and came back only for him to do it again. Don't fight him back I kept telling myself. When I came to this time I was on the ground and spit was coming down on me.

"Stop!" I heard in the distance "I'm going to call the police.

He walked back over to the car and drove off as if nothing happened. I reached for my phone to call Nautica. She arrived the same time   as   the   ambulance.

"You need to press charges," the nurse that called the police kept saying, "He is never going to stop
and this is just the beginning baby."

As I laid in the hospital, the police kept asking if I wanted to press charges. They took my report, but I was confused. Maybe I deserve it? After all, I had prayed for this man and I wasn't exactly innocent.

The next day he sent his family to come and get his belongings from my apartment. How dare he attack me and now send his family to my house? He accused me of keeping his check that he was under the impression had come to my house. His accusations led me to become enraged. So, enraged that I took what was left in my house and cut his watch up, threw all his clothes in the floor and bleached them. For three days I couldn't swallow solids because of him choking me.

I wish I could say it ended there, but it didn't. I linked back up with Mr. Wrong for a about a month, but I realized it wasn't healthy to be with him; I was broken. Eventually Mr. Wrong-too and I got back together, and he proposed one night at the same place where he choked and threw me on the ground. He had music playing from his car and he got down on one knee. He apologized for everything he had done,

"How can we make it work?" He asked.

I was so surprised. Deep down this was all I wanted from him, but I knew it wasn't time.

"We can't. I can't marry you."

For the first time I saw real pain in his eyes. I felt so bad that during my lunch break I went over to his house and apologized to him. He asked again, and I accepted.

I thought our relationship was going to finally take a turn for the better. We began to plan our wedding, but something didn't feel right.

"God if this is truly the man you want me to be with," I prayed one night as I laid next to him, "Give me some type of sign."

He began to become more controlling and even though he was still cheating, we moved in together. The house was 30 minutes from campus, no one would come to visit me. He had finally isolated me. I called off the wedding several times.

He promised that he would never put his hands on me again, but he became emotionally abusive.

"All your friends are jealous of you, they just don't want to see you happy" he would say to me every time we would get into a disagreement.

If I questioned him about anything he would turn   in   on   me,

"You are so jealous and insecure."

I was at the end of my rope with him. One day he came home, and I overheard him talking on the phone to a female.

"She isn't nothing and I don't really even care about her,"

I knew then it was time for me to go.

Niece, me on again, off again friend, was currently in school at UAB. I knew she didn't like him and she knew I wanted out of that situation. I would miss class to look for an apartment in Birmingham even though I knew I couldn't afford one on my own. I'm not sure what came over me, but on this tour, I explained to the lady the situation.

"Don't worry about a thing sweetie, the apartment is   yours."

I knew he would find out sooner or later that I was planning on leaving him. A couple days after the securing my new apartment I came home to him on my computer again.

"Are you planning on leaving me?" he asked

Already knowing the answer. I told him "yes" and we began to have an argument. It ended with him standing over me, yelling and accusing me of not being faithful. I explained to him that this was best for the both of us and that I overheard his conversation with the girl on the phone telling her that I wasn't anything to him. He yelled back,

"It's because of Idaguy isn't it?"

He had gone through an old sim card and saw our messages. Knowing it was partially true I didn't respond. Idaguy was my voice of reasoning, so yes, I still talked to him. He knew everything about the relationship between Mr. Wrong-too and myself. I was all geared up to move until I caught the flu. Up until this point Mr. Wrong-Too and I were trying to have a baby, not the smartest idea I know which I is why had begun going to the health center to have "the shot" injections. Deep down I knew that I did not want to be with him my entire life. Having a baby would ensure this nightmare never come to an end.

When the day came for me to move we had sex one last time. I'll admit moving to Birmingham was very lonely, I didn't know anyone here and didn't have time to meet anyone because I was still driving back and forth to finish up my last year of college. One night the loneliness got to me and I asked him to come and see me. We started sleeping together again, but because there was no trust I insisted he use a condom. Not wanting to be judged for sleeping with him again, I hid our relationship.

November 7, 2010, I found out I was pregnant. I was so upset with myself! How out of all people could I allow myself to get pregnant by this fool? I escaped from him one time, but still I found myself in the situation. A glimmer of hope crossed my heart because a month prior Idaguy had come to visit. I called Idaguy to explain to him what was going on. He was so excited, he explained to me that during sex he had taken the condom off and went all the way with me. Furious doesn't explain how I felt. Putting it back on me he immediately became defensive,

"V you knew what happened because it felt different."

Mr. Wrong-too had denied getting me pregnant and he was right, now I had to go back and tell him that he was right, it could be someone else.

Mr. Wrong-too as expected was upset when I told him.

I asked him for money to get an abortion, but he refused.

"No, Vic I told you that we were always going to be together and you're not going to kill my baby."

I made an appointment to the clinic for an abortion. At the appointment, the lady made me feel so guilty about the decision that I changed my mind.

Not knowing what to do, I quit my job with the state at the hospital and with no steady income how could I take care of a baby. Mr. Wrong-too wasn't taking care of his first child so I knew things weren't going to be different this time. I spent days on the couch crying, trying to pop pills to make myself sick enough to miscarry. My life felt as if it was coming to an end, fast in a hurry.

I should have listened to my instincts. I should have followed my first mind in many of the situations that I have accounted for in this story, but the truth is, I ignored it for what seemed convenient, comfortable, profitable, and satisfying for the moment. However, as you also can see, ignoring the Holy Spirit that God put inside of you leads to hurt, pain, regret, and sorrow. Listen to and discipline yourself to not press the limits on something that you know is not healthy. I played the edge so many times in my past that I could be dead and gone, but God. It's good to play the edge when it's for a good cause, but not when you are playing with fire because you will always get burned.

One day the tears you cry will all be worth it.

Suicide is the 10th leading cause of death in the U.S.

13 SUICIDES

As I said before, I have been different all my life. Not really belonging to the, "in crowd," but not an outcast either. After I ended things with Mr. Wrong-too, I found myself in a whirlwind of problems. I began to question myself, always wondering if I was good enough. See unlike physical abuse, the effects of psychological abuse linger long after the bruises are gone.

I remember it as if it was yesterday. I was headed to the orthodontist and I needed him to watch our daughter, Lady. Funny thing is, when he arrived to meet me, he wasn't in his car. I knew then this day was going to end up going south. Everything he had been telling me was a lie. Immediately I felt that I was allowing myself to be put back in the same situation I had crawled away from. He could tell that I was enraged with him, but right now was not the time to argue. I had an appointment to make and quite frankly, I was tired of going back and forth with him. now was not the time to argue. I had an appointment to make and quite frankly I was tired of going back and forth with him.

I was tired of all his bull crap and manipulation. I gave him Lady and headed to my appointment. I guess I was more shaken than I thought because the dental assistant kept asking me if I was okay. Like always I said I was okay and like always I was crying on the inside, feeling as if my life was being ripped apart for the thousandth time

When I went to pick up Lady, he called me "her" name. I stood in disbelief. His lies had finally caught up with him. He tried to convince me that this wasn't her car, but I had already spotted the shoes on the backseat. As I was pulling out, she pulled up in his car and a quick glance, which felt like hours, caused me to think to myself that this can't be what my life has come to.

I cried the entire way home. I sent text messages because surely, he had a reasonable explanation for what happened and like always he lied. His lies beget more lies and that night, June 20, 2012, I decided enough was enough. I was tired. I was emotionally drained with nothing left to give. I could no longer handle what life was throwing at me. Luckily my brother was in town, so I asked him to watch the baby while I went for a ride to clear my head. He looked shocked because she was only two, but I trusted him. He agreed, and I left.

Unbeknownst to him, I had taken a couple of Lortabs and was contemplating killing myself, but I didn't want to go without reaching out for one last attempt at love. I sent out a few text messages to see who would respond. Ugh! The one who replied was not one I really wanted to link up with, but in this moment, it was better than nothing. I needed something, anything to get me over what I was feeling. The entire drive from 65 to 20/59, I continuously thought about if I wanted to really be bothered with him. Our history was garbage and honestly, I wasn't attracted to him at all.

I'm not sure how we met, all I know is that he was on a social media site back in 2006. He was super attracted to me and I had little to no interest in him at all. However, whenever I called, texted or sent a bird with a message, he was right there without a second thought, like tonight. He knew of my lack of attraction to him and I know it bothered him, but for whatever reason he would still allow me to pick him up and throw him down at my leisure. I wonder why, but that's another book for another time.

Arriving at his house I instantly felt sick. What was I doing? My mind didn't want this, my body didn't want this. When he came to the door I was immediately turned off even more. What the hell was I thinking? I don't deserve this, he doesn't deserve this. Why am I giving him a false sense of hope, this would never be more than it always has been. I was doing to him what others had done to me. I immediately texted my friend,

"I don't want to be here anymore, I'm tired of life, I'm tired of not being loved, I'm tired of men lying to me to see what they could get from me. I'm tired." The day before my tire was low and I had put air in it several times. It continued to leak, but like always I didn't have the money to do anything other than bandage it up. Sort of like my life. I always bandaged it up when it really needed to be cleaned out, so it could heal properly. I recall looking over and seeing a gas station to my left, "I should put air in it again before I get on the interstate," I told myself. But whatever! I was still high from the night before and nothing mattered anymore. I headed for the interstate prepared to fight the morning traffic. No more than two minutes later, my car began to swerve out of control. "Jesus!" I screamed as I grabbed a hold of the steering wheel. I wasn't ready to die despite my previous sentiments. The car swerved again, this time to the left before flipping three times and landing arm's length from oncoming traffic. It hit me that earlier that day my car had been smoking so I knew I needed to get out.

An ambulance arrived, and the medics place me on a gurney. One would think that right now my thoughts are thanking God I'm still alive, but it wasn't. As I lay there I remembered I had pills in my purse and with the police standing over me I began to get nervous. "Can they tell I'm high?" I thought to myself. "I can't go to jail, I can't lose my baby." I reached in the purse and dropped the pills on the ground. I'll never knew if they saw them, but I do know God again had grace and mercy on me.

I was taken to UAB and later that night the therapist came in to do a psych evaluation on me.

"You're suffering from depression," he said you should really think about seeking therapy." In my mind, I didn't think there was anything wrong with me. I just need to regroup and reflect I told myself.

My family wanted to move home, but that wasn't an option. I wanted to be nowhere near them. Pull it together Vic, I kept telling myself. I needed to get out of Alabama.

Idaguy and I had a DNA test that he was not the father and he was hurt after the results confirmed my daughter was not his baby. Event still we decided to work on us. However, upon moving to VA it was apparent to both of us that we were better off as friend.

I moved back to Alabama after 5 months, and it was shortly after that Mr. Wrong-too and I started sleeping with one another again.

I wasn't mentally stable, I had gotten evicted and I felt like a terrible mother. My daughter deserved better than what I was putting her through. I had a good job, but I wasn't properly managing my money. So again, I turned to what I knew, and I started dating another guy. We were more like friends, but I could depend on him for anything. "This is it for me," I thought. He had five children including one that wasn't his biologically, but he treated them as if they were and I admired that about him.

Everything was going well until he lost his job. Being a provider, it really affected him mentally. I wanted him to know that it was not about the money, so I assured him I wasn't going anywhere. He couldn't seem to understand that. We had been together three months and with the recent financial strain, I told him it was best for me to get back on birth control. Before I could make it to my appointment the next week he called me,

"I went to the clinic," he said, "and I have contracted something."

My mind was in disbelief, I asked him if he was having any symptoms. When he told me his testcases were tender. I immediately flashed back to Mr. Wrong-Too. Not wanting to overreact I called my doctor and told her the situation. I went in to see her that day.

"How in the world did this happen? Why am I getting punished for trying to do right?" I cried to my friend Nautica. "I haven't cheated, or have I entertained anyone."

As I lay on the table, legs propped open butt hanging off she told me that she didn't see anything. What! I sat straight up in the middle of the exam. "Are you sure?" I asked. "Yes, but I will still send this to the lab just to be on the safe side." I was pissed, I was hurt and again I didn't understand how or why I was in this situation.

Three days later I called the doctor's office for my results and they were negative. I drove up there to get a printout then I called Mooney, "I want to come see you at work." I was ready to light his ass up.

I knew exactly where to find him because he worked where I used to live. As he walked down the stairs I didn't speak. "Are you sure I'm the only one you've been sleeping with?" I asked as I began to read my test results. "NEGATIVE! I'm negative of EVERYTHING." At this time, I noticed that his eye was pink.

"I guess that hoe you messing with got you in your eye too."

"That's mean Victoria, I woke up with a sty on my eye."

"You only get them when you lie," I snarled at him.

I couldn't hold it in anymore. I started to cry. "What did I do to make you lie to me? Am I that bad of a person? Did I not do everything you wanted me to do?" Nonchalantly he looked at me and said, "Calm down," as he walked off. I put my car in drive and hit the gas. I tried my best to hit him with my car, but he jumped out of the way.

For a week I couldn't eat nor sleep. Trying to stay focused I went to work like nothing ever happened. I tried to keep a smile on my face. No one knew I was popping pills, no one knew I was drinking every night. Mr. Wrong-too was getting on my nerves, he refused to take care of our daughter and Mooney was still holding on to that same tired lie that his job was making him work crazy hours. I had gone back to church, but nothing the pastor said was speaking to me. I was tired again! I wanted out.

It was a Wednesday night and I picked up some pills from a friend and grabbed a beer before heading to drop my daughter off with Nautica. I parked around the corner and reflected on my life all the while popping pills and sipping on my drink. After three pills and a beer, I decided I wanted my baby. I could barely see while driving home.

When we arrived home, I tried to put my daughter to bed, but for some reason she kept getting out.

Lady was only three, but I found myself getting upset because when I would wake up she had moved my beer. This happened three times. The last time she laid on top of me and I couldn't reach it. Finally, I went to sleep. The next morning, I woke up as if nothing happened and took Lady to daycare and picked up my work children for their appointments all while nursing a hangover.

"You guys are always late. We are going to cancel all the appointments."

I heard the lady behind the desk say as I signed my clients in. I explained to her that we had never been here before, she apologized,

"I thought you all were with another agency."

I sat in the waiting room falling in and out of sleep trying to hold back the tears of my life.

After the appointment, I took the boys back to the office, I could barely walk straight. I sat in the hallway chair and began to cry. One of the therapist called me back to her office to talk.

"Are you okay?" I remember her asking. So tired. All I could do was utter, "I am tired." Knowing something was wrong she called Nautica and informed her that she needed to go and get my daughter from daycare. She and another therapist escorted me out the backdoor to Brookwood Hospital where I was admitted for 3 days and 4 nights.

My first night was pure hell, one of my previous co- workers was there doing intakes and another was working as an aid. "What you are doing here?" they both asked, "I always thought you had it all together."

This is what I didn't want to deal with, being judged. They pumped me with so many pills, until I couldn't go to the bathroom. I was resistant and didn't want to participate in any sessions. My daughter couldn't come visit me because she was to young, this caused me to have an outburst which resulted in me being further drugged and threatened to have my days extended.

"I'm not like these other people." I kept telling myself. "I have my stuff together." Some of the people there used it as a pit stop for pills, girls would share stories on how they tried to swallow forks to get admitted, there were even couples here together. I knew what I had to do to get out, tell them what they wanted to hear. "I feel bad, I'll never do it again." I really thought it was going to be that easy, thank God it wasn't.

My next session with my psychiatrist included him asking me how I was doing. "Great!" I said as I tried to crack a smile.

"How are you adjusting to your meds?" he asked. "I don't like them, I can't go to the bathroom."

When he asked if I thought I should be discharged, I hurriedly replied yes! Looking up from my file he said,

"No, you're not. You're still trying to convince me you don't need help and because of that it is my recommendation that you stay a while longer."

Knowing that nothing I said was going to work I just nodded my head and said okay. I was pissed beyond words. When I walked out of that office I fell to my knees and began to cry. The nursing staff threatened to restrain me if I didn't get myself together and stop.

I had an array of emotions going through me. No one had come to see me, I couldn't see my baby, my mom only called once and even then, she wasn't understanding, and I could tell she had made no real effort to come and see me. I felt so alone. No one cared. I was abandoned and all I could do was talk to the four walls.

Had it gotten so bad that this is what the result was? To be honest, as I reflect, this visit to the hospital was due to years and years and years of toxic, poisonous build up in my life. Not once was I 100% comfortable with risky lifestyle that I was living, but I never saw it as something that I needed to seek help for. Listen people, this is not normal.

Up until this point the fact that I kept accepting less than for my life was not normal, but I normalized it. I didn't seek help because quite honestly, I didn't know that I needed to. I thought I was unhappy. It wasn't until later that I realized I was addicted to sex and the many benefits that came with it. Using it as means to an end. I should have had an intervention at an early age, but it took an accumulation of events to bring me to this point and realize that this indeed was not normal, and I needed a change. It didn't make me feel good about myself neither did it make me a better person. It didn't add to me, but the lifestyle I was living surely knew how to subtract.

ACKNOWLEDGE
ACCEPT &
AFFIRM

14 WHO AM I...?

Grandmothers, mothers, and daughters I know this wasn't the book that you thought you were going to read, but it is the story that needed to be told. I know you may have thought this was going to be how a little girl was too fast and hot in the pants and learned her lesson one day and yes that's partially true, but as you can see there is so much more to it than that.

This book was meant to inspire you to pay attention to your daughters and the things that they are going through. Raising a child today is so hard especially with the social media influences and people having children younger and younger.

It isn't fair that we must lose ourselves to find ourselves again.

This book is for you to understand that we shouldn't have to die to live again.

I went through so much and this is just the half of it. I felt that love was going to come in the form of a man in a bed instead of loving myself first. From men to women to drugs and alcohol, losing cars and homes. I pray no one must do the most to find love when **love lies within God and God alone.** No man or woman should ever make you feel less than what you are. God makes no mistakes, you are perfect in all your ways and if you listen your imperfections make you **imperfectly   perfect.**

When you see your sister, struggling don't judge her or write it off as if she is being just her and in another one of her mood swings. Ask her questions. Study her behaviors. Know her triggers because when she needs you the most she might not saying anything until it's too late.

I thank God that He strategically placed people in my life that loved and cared for me despite all my ups and downs. Depression, suicide and being very promiscuous isn't healthy!

We need to stop being afraid to talk about our hurt and allow healthy help to come in. Sometimes a simple, "I will be there for you," can and will go a long way.

I'm interested to know what you think! After reading my story alone, with a child or in a book club, what are your thoughts? Are there situations you found eerily like your own life? Do you have things you are unsure about in your life and you want feedback? Jot them down here and reach out to me at www.victorianlong.com to share!

Join my group online:
She's Confident w/ Victoria Necole
(bit.ly/shesconfident)!

Love you!

CONVERSATION WITH A CLINICIAN:

After writing this book I sat down for a conversation with KD Reid, Freedom Strategist and Women's Empowerment Counselor to get her perspectives and what she hoped the take-a-ways would be.

***

As a clinician, what I hope that you take away from this book is that sexual abuse, rape and molestation are real. Even if you keep sweeping it under the rug or out the door, it is real. The effects of sexual violations are real. Many people who are promiscuous, bitter, rude and "out there" as we like to say, are only acting out based on their experiences. Did you know every 8 minutes child protective services substantiates a claim of child sexual abuse, 34% of all victims are under the age of 12. Perpetrators of child sexual abuse are often related to the victim with 80% being a parent and 6% being other relatives.

Many times, people are unsure of how their childhood affects their current state or situations they have been in. I know it is cliché, but it's true our childhood is the foundation of our lives. If you or anyone you know have been affected by sexual abuse, deal with unreconciled issues stemming from childhood or feel lost and stuck in life, reach out for help! Therapy works, and we must erase the stigma in our communities that it doesn't. I hope that you take away the fact that there are other types of abuse outside of physical. There is emotional and psychological and in every case the ramifications are far greater. This abuse not only affects you but those around you whether it be children or friends.

As a Christian, what I hope that you will take away from this book is that everything we experience in life is not a direct result of our lack of faith. Everyone who is engaging in behaviors you wouldn't or that you have forgotten that you used to, isn't hell bound. Reach out to them! Talk to them, not at them. Listen to what they say and don't say. Pray with them and then refer them to a professional. Prayer is an amazing thing. It is a privilege to be able to approach God for ourselves, but He has also given us earthly resources in which to act after praying: doctors, therapists, and coaches. Seek out one or all of them to better your life or the life of someone else!

As a mother, what I hope that you take away from this book is to always be aware of your child's surroundings. So often we teach our children to watch out for stranger danger when we need to teach them to be aware of those they know as well. We as parents must be mindful of our interactions with our children for they create or close the doorway to communication. We won't catch everything, and when we don't we have to forgive ourselves, but the things we don't catch or pick up on, we want to make sure our babies regardless of age, feel comfortable talking to us about it. Never forget how things were when you were that age and imagine it being 10x harder for your child due to the advancement of society. Love on your kids and ask questions. Every behavior is a statement of communication to the world and most importantly to us.

As a woman, what I hope that you take away from this book, is we all have a story to tell. We have all had one, two or all these men in our lives. Each person we engage with, deposits something in us whether it be positive or negative. Every person we encounter has a lesson for us to learn. If we are honest we haven't always been grown and mature, we haven't always been Christians and we haven't always exhibited self- respect. I hope that you learn to see beyond the actions and behaviors of others and even their choices and seek to understand what they are saying with the words they don't speak. If you are a woman who finds yourself in a situation like this don't be ashamed to reach out and seek professional help. Seek help reconciling the issues from your past that keep you from living a life of freedom and address the roadblocks that keep you from being liberated.

ABOUT THE AUTHOR

Chapter Her life, business, and story can be likened to an excellent Lifetime movie filled with all the elements needed to make it a number one seller. Drama, suspense, horror, surprise, happiness, and yes even comedy is what keeps you on the edge of your seat every time she shares her story to empower other women and children to overcome through confessing their stories. The details of her journey carry you through a range of emotions and you always leave this young lady captivated once you meet her.

Victoria Long is not a victim, but a "victor" of domestic violence, sexual abuse, and suicide. She is the proud mother of Kaytlyn "Lady" Delani, 2nd oldest of four siblings to Shirley Long, member of Kingdom Builders in Birmingham, AL., under the covering of Milton Wren Jr., the owner of a non-profit organization called, "The Confessions of a Lady" established in August of 2015. She is also the author of, *10 Ways to Cope with Depression.* Where yet again she has taken her pain to help others to overcome.

She knows that she is alive today for the sole purpose of spreading the message of

Psalm 139:14 which states, *"I will praise You, for I am fearfully and wonderfully made; Marvelous are Your works, and that my soul knows very well"* – NKJV. During prayer and meditation, she sought the Lord for guidance in her life and this is the Scripture that God branded in her heart. From this Divine intervention, she shares the message given to her by God, "Your imperfections make you perfect, you are imperfectly perfect!"

Born in Wichita and raised in Junction City, Kansas, she moved to Florida at the age of 13. She continued her journey to Alabama, becoming a graduate of the University of Alabama in Tuscaloosa with a degree in Human Environmental Sciences. She is currently a member of the Birmingham Urban league of Young Professionals and one of the recipients of the 2017 Young Progressive Black Caucus of Alabama Women of Color and Leadership Award.

You can find Victoria hosting events for, "The Confessions of a Lady." She hosted her inaugural women's conference, "Imperfectly Perfect," in October of 2015, her second, "Imperfectly Perfect - Know Your Worth," February of 2016 and has served as a guest speaker at various

events and schools. Her first
Fashion Show, "Love after War,"
was March of 2017. She is fully
committed to the journey of helping
other women that have gone
through similar circumstances and
embracing all things fashionably
lady like.

Victoria is a Confidence Coach where she
helps women to acknowledge their past,
accept that they can't change it and affirm
themselves that they're deserving of a
better, brighter and greater future!

Made in the USA
Columbia, SC
21 March 2018